THE ACCEPTANCE OF HISTORIES

Toward a Perspective for
Social Science

BY

KENNETH E. BOCK

UNIVERSITY OF CALIFORNIA PRESS
BERKELEY AND LOS ANGELES
1956

University of California Publications in Sociology and Social Institutions

Editors: Reinhard Bendix, Wolfram Eberhard, Philip Selznick

Volume 3, No. 1, pp. 1–132

Submitted by editors June 17, 1955
Issued March 28, 1956
Price, $1.75

University of California Press
Berkeley and Los Angeles
California

❖

Cambridge University Press
London, England

FOREWORD

THIS ESSAY had its beginnings in the writer's doctoral dissertation, "The Comparative Method." Further reflection on that limited theme and a more extended exploration of the theory of historical inquiry involved has suggested a more broadly conceived exposition of the ideas underlying the effort to institute a historical science of society and culture. Thus, from an originally critical enterprise an attempt to construct a perspective for social science has arisen.

Although I must assume responsibility for the views expressed here, I am conscious, nevertheless, of a substantial indebtedness to others. My basic obligation to the late Professor Frederick J. Teggart will be apparent to all those who know his work. In their guidance and suggestions on earlier phases of the manuscript, Professors George H. Hildebrand and Theodore D. McCown contributed richly to my education. Conversations with Professor Edward W. Strong over a long period have introduced me to the various intricacies of a theory of history and have provided me with some awareness, I must hope, of the hazardous character of this enterprise. To Professor Margaret T. Hodgen, for her constant encouragement, friendship, and scholarly assistance and example during the past twenty years, I owe thanks that cannot be properly or adequately expressed in prefatory remarks.

The manuscript in substantially completed form has been read by Professors Herbert Blumer, Carle C. Zimmerman, and A. Irving Hallowell, and I am grateful for their assistance in clarifying several points as well as for their friendly encouragement.

The members of the Editorial Committee of the University of California Press series in Sociology and Social Institutions, Professors Reinhard Bendix, Wolfram Eberhard, and Philip Selznick, have offered many valuable suggestions for final revision of the manuscript. I acknowledge with thanks their patient and generous assistance.

The expert editing by Mr. John Gildersleeve of the University of California Press has produced a large measure of whatever clarity readers may find in the text; surviving obscurities testify to the protective instinct that a stubborn writer shows for his own words.

A part of the research leading to this publication has been carried out under a grant from the Institute of Social Sciences of the University of California.

CONTENTS

INTRODUCTION

FRUITFUL INQUIRY in any field begins with a recognition and specification of problems in current explication of observed phenomena.

This requirement cannot be met in the social studies simply by the gross judgment that we have been ignorant or mistaken with respect to the broad questions we set ourselves. It is not enough that we seek to cleanse our minds, in Cartesian fashion, by an act of will, and then proceed to write truly on the *tabula rasa*. If a science finds itself in trouble, the first obligation is to ascertain just what the trouble is, and then to go about correcting it in the light of that analysis. A science cannot escape its past by ignoring it.

A specification of present problems in the social sciences, and an effort to meet them, calls, then, for historical recognition of the way we have come to this present and for an inspection of the intellectual baggage we have acquired along the way. We cannot, and we do not, approach our current tasks with a blank mind; a complex heritage of ideas persistently invades the mythical arena wherein pure reason seeks to do fresh battle with old questions. Failure to recognize that heritage places us in perpetual servitude to it and blocks the enfranchisement of mind required for the creative act.

Historical study of ideas serves a need that cannot be met by merely critical or logical analysis. Although it is in the context of current habits of thought that we must seek the problems from which inquiry can take its departure, the present is not an open book. The ideas to which we pay conscious homage are not necessarily those that most strongly guide our thinking. The didactically given conceptual framework often gives no expression to the basic world view that dictates its outlines. There is, in Dewey's words, a "familiar furniture of the mind" which, just because it is common stock, passes unnoticed and is allowed to exert an unsuspected tyranny over what we confidently regard as the liberal flow of our reason. But what is only implicit in one epoch of thought is explicit in another, so that by looking back and finding open expression of ideas that now lurk darkly at the borders of our awareness we can come to understand better the content of our heritage and the service or disservice it may do us.

The following study is an essay in the history of ideas. It seeks a specification of the difficulties attending present efforts to depict social or cultural processes and suggests ways of meeting those difficulties. The burden of the argument is that we have inherited a comprehensive theory of social change based on an analogy between society and an

[1]

organism; that traditional conceptions of the "nature" of human experience have introduced a dichotomy between what takes place regularly or in accordance with "law" and what happens by chance, or accidentally; that this dualism has been responsible for the use of methods by which process is sought outside the context of what is regarded as the historically "unique"; and, consequently, that the foundations of empirical inquiry into social and cultural processes must lie in an acceptance of experience as historically given, without gratuitous distinctions between the "natural" and "accidental" as they are identified by an *a priori* theory of change.

The order in which this argument is developed calls for a word of explanation. Attention is directed first to the nineteenth century. One aim is to recall that in the formative years of sociology and anthropology the value of a historical perspective was clearly recognized. The problems involved in pursuing a historical science were directly faced at that time, and the difficulties introduced by the adoption of certain ideas of how the objective was to be reached are more apparent than at a later date. The purpose here is not to reveal the superficial deficiencies of the so-called comparative-historical method characteristic of nineteenth-century inquiry, but to seek a clue to the fundamental ideas that prescribed such a procedure and that continue to influence our efforts to elicit statements of historical processes.

The nineteenth century can serve here as a pivot for exposition. Once we discard the notion that the comparative-historical method of the period was only a "curious aberration of thought," we are at once led to a search for an explanation of the tenacious grip it had on the minds of able men earnestly pursuing a science of society. This explanation is sought in the historical background explored in Part II.

A return to the more immediate present in Part III reveals not only a widespread continued adherence to particular methods of nineteenth-century inquiry but, more important, a persistent devotion to the basic outlook responsible for those methods. It is in this context that a reformulation of perspective is attempted.

PART ONE

The Nineteenth-Century Science of History

CHAPTER I

THE HISTORICAL ORIENTATION OF EARLY SOCIOLOGY

AT ITS INCEPTION as a discipline in the nineteenth century, sociology aimed at a reconstruction of society that would rescue the individual from his recent isolation by bringing him into a system of group relations that would act as a buffer between him and incomprehensible Leviathan. Conscious concern with accumulated dislocations following upon the disruption of a legendary medieval order was accompanied, however, by a deep conviction that the social needs of men could be satisfied neither by utopian schemes for the building of an ideal republic nor by the legislative fiat of revolutionary governments.

The task of sociology was more broadly conceived to involve a scientific demonstration of the basic conditions of social order and, above all, of the processes through which those conditions gradually developed. Social change through time thus became the main focus of interest, and the objective was not simply to advocate a program of directed change but to discover natural laws of change that could serve as guides in social reorganization. Sociology was to be a *historical* science.

The methods employed in this great project and the ideas that informed it are not singular aberrations of nineteenth-century thought. Closer examination will show that they were even then deeply rooted in Western social theory and that they continue to exert an often unsuspected influence on contemporary thought. The object in this chapter is to present an exposition of these ideas as they are represented in the work of Auguste Comte, Herbert Spencer, and John Stuart Mill, influential forerunners of modern sociology.

AUGUSTE COMTE (1798–1857)

Although the ultimate objective of Comte's positive philosophy was a "regeneration of society," he felt that this could be accomplished only after the European position in the developmental cultural series had been determined and it had been discovered "by what necessary chain of successive transformations the human race, starting from a condition barely superior to that of a society of great apes, has been gradually led up to the present stage of European civilization."[1] This demanded,

---

[1] Auguste Comte, *System of Positive Polity*, trans. by John H. Bridges, *et al.* (London, 1875–1877), I:32–36; "Philosophical Considerations on the Sciences and Savants," *ibid.*, IV:599.

according to Comte's definition of the term, a historical approach to the study of society.

When he examined the way in which the study of the past had been conducted up to his time, however, Comte was convinced that traditional procedures could never yield truly scientific results. Historians were mere annalists or chroniclers who, guided by a superficial philosophy and preoccupied with the incidental or the accidental, made the world a "scene of miracles" in which great men or divine intervention shaped the course of events. Given this outlook, historians could do no more than produce concrete narratives, and the result was invariably a form of literature, not science.

The difficulty, as Comte saw it, lay in the fact that historians had concentrated on data of a kind that was simply not amenable to scientific treatment. Particular events, specific situations, and the deeds of individual men could not be manipulated conceptually to yield laws of social development. Attention had to be directed elsewhere, to those underlying "forces" that "produced" events or to the "natural progress" of society that determined the particular advances of any period.[2]

Comte's proposed method for a scientific study of history can best be understood by noting the intimate relationship in which he placed sociology and biology in his hierarchy of the sciences. Sociology, as he conceived it, dealt with an order of phenomena strictly analogous to the organisms studied by biologists. Social statics, a study of the order and functions of society, paralleled anatomy in the life sciences. Social dynamics was the sociological equivalent of physiology. The process of social change was to be regarded, consequently, as a development or growth in the biological sense.

In view of these parallels, Comte felt justified in looking to biology for methodological guidance in the new science of sociology. He regarded the comparative method as the chief mode of biological inquiry, and it was therefore thought appropriate to a study of society. This method, he observed, involved a rational comparison of different independent coexisting states of human society scattered over the earth. The procedure also suggested a temporal relationship among the items compared, for it furnished a device for observing, in the present, earlier stages in the growth of modern civilization. By virtue of a peculiar— and unexplained—concatenation of circumstances, Comte argued, every possible degree of social evolution is represented by some existing people. Between the lowly inhabitants of Tierra del Fuego and the

---

[2] For Comte's critique of the traditional historian, see his "Plan of the Scientific Operations Necessary for Reorganizing Society," *ibid.*, IV:556–559, 587–588.

most advanced peoples of Western Europe every imaginable shade of social development could be found in some observable society. Not only was the comparative method a device for recovering origins; it could play an active part in reconstructing the entire historical record.[3] It was apparently necessary only to arrange a spatial distribution of social or cultural differences in the proper sequence in order to arrive at a picture of what the temporal progress from savagery to civilization had been.

It should be recalled that Comte's attention was centered on Western Europe; it was the history of that civilization that he sought to depict. The question immediately arises, then, as to how the condition of one society—that of Tierra del Fuego, for example—can be presented as evidence in a reconstruction of the history of another, such as that of Western Europe. Comte did not hesitate to face this problem, for it appeared to him that an unassailable axiom justified the procedure. This was the well-established fact that there is a constant and necessary identity in the fundamental development of mankind, which flows in turn from the uniformity of human nature. Human progress is a function of human nature, Comte maintained, and since the latter is stable the progress cannot be altered. Thus it is "the fundamental laws of the human organization" that account for the striking similarity of the customs of early Greece to those of present North American Indians, or of the feudal Malays to the peoples of eleventh-century Europe.[4] Since all peoples must pass through essentially the same stages of development, it follows that the progress of an advanced people can be documented by reference to the status of other, less advanced peoples.[5]

It must be noted, however, that Comte was by no means satisfied with either the comparative method or the use of laws of human nature as tools for the scientific study of history. The comparative method was, after all, primarily suited to biology, not sociology. Comte recognized clearly that a mere arrangement of ethnographic data could not, alone, tell us anything about temporal succession. Members of the series did not fall automatically into a time order. The method yielded a coexistent,

---

[3] Auguste Comte, *Cours de Philosophie Positive*, 4ᵉ ed. (Paris, 1877), IV:318.

[4] *Ibid.*, IV:318–319, 558; *Positive Polity*, III:532; "Plan of the Scientific Operations," IV:556–557. The point is worth emphasizing in view of recent claims that the classical evolutionists did not actually insist on parallel development.

[5] Comte recognized, of course, that all peoples had not passed through the same stages *simultaneously*. The fact that they had not is what made the use of the comparative method possible. Comte handled the problem of cultural differences by asserting that special racial, climatic, and political factors had operated—apparently fortuitously—to vary the *speed* of progress in different societies but not the basic *course* of progress. See *Cours*, IV:284–285, 317–318; "Plan of the Scientific Operations," IV:537.

rather than a consecutive, series. Again, it was not a distinctly sociological procedure to try to derive history from laws of human nature, which were regarded by Comte as a subject of biological investigation. Succeeding generations influenced each other to such a degree, he felt, that it was impossible to deduce the history of man from the nature of man.

It was in the light of these reservations concerning ethnography and psychology (biology) that Comte introduced the "historical method," which he described as forming the very core of his positive philosophy and comprising the sociological method *par excellence.*[6]

The historical method, according to Comte, aims at the construction of a developmental social series. If we are to discern this series, if we are to avoid the confused descriptions offered by ordinary historians, if we are not to be lost in a sterile empiricism, then we must *begin* with a "leading rational conception" of human development or social evolution. Some broad view of history must be adopted, Comte insisted, if the different periods of civilizational growth are to be seen as stages in a general evolution. In fact, it was the rational subordination of humanity to a single law of continuous development that gave to positivism its "exclusive and spontaneous character."[7]

True to his own admonition, Comte reached, very early in his career, a general notion of what the course of history had been, and this continued to serve him throughout subsequent inquiries. Civilization, he wrote in 1822, progresses according to a necessary law. This course is natural and inevitable since it results from the nature of human nature. There could be no dispute about this, in Comte's opinion, for "all men who possess a certain knowledge of the leading facts of history . . . will agree in this, that the cultivated portion of the human race, considered as a whole, has made uninterrupted progress in civilization from the most remote periods of history to our own day." The progress, moreover, has followed a strictly determined order of succession, and it has displayed "a remarkable fixity which manifests an essentially exact similitude as between parallel developments."[8]

Comte regarded all this as an "elementary conception of social dynamics," a given starting-point in the search for a law that would describe the process in detail. Following Condorcet, Comte felt that this law should depict the experience of a hypothetical single people to whom all the consecutive phases of social development observed among separate nations could be referred. He thought it unnecessary to con-

---

[6] *Cours,* IV:321–323.
[7] *Ibid.,* IV:135–136, 324.
[8] "Plan of the Scientific Operations," IV:555–556; *Cours,* IV:265–266.

sider the entire social development, however, since all aspects of human existence—physical, moral, intellectual, or political—moved in a fixed and simultaneous order. Thus it was possible to abstract any one of these elements, follow its course, and so arrive at the general social development. Since Comte believed that the intellectual factor was preponderant among these interconnected aspects, he attended to it alone, and his law of history accordingly turned out to be his well-known law of the three stages of intellectual development.

An outstanding feature, therefore, of Comte's scientific history was that it was to be conceived and written in the abstract. This meant not only that attention should be focused on a single series and on intellectual development within that series, but also that a science of history would consider the progress of only the most advanced peoples, avoiding any digressions on other societies whose development had been, *par des causes quelconques,* stopped in an imperfect state. The study could be confined, in other words, to *l'avant-garde de l'humanité,* the white people of Western Europe. Nor did abstraction stop here. Comte argued further that in the search for historical laws all "exceptional events" and insignificant details should be discarded, and that, ideally, true history could be written without using the names of individual men or even of peoples. Finally, all historical data were to be carefully sorted, and those that appeared to be of secondary importance—for example, circumstances of climate or locality—must be discarded as not in keeping with the demands of an abstract science.[9]

Since, for Comte, the principal objective of a scientific history was the delineation of a series of stages in social development, a crucial step in the procedure was the division of history into epochs. What we are given in historical records is merely a sequence of happenings or an account of successive situations and conditions. How are these discrete phenomena to be sorted and characterized as epochs? Here Comte stated simply that he followed the example of Condorcet and achieved a division "through philosophic observation of the past,"[10] "a first sketch of the synoptic view, a first *coup d'oeil* over the general history of civilization." If the question be raised as to just what would be observed in this procedure, we note that Comte returned to "histories heretofore written," which he accepted as a "tolerable equivalent" for a first collection of data.[11]

It appears, then, that in Comte's peculiar conception of the historical method the need for a detailed study of what had happened was obvi-

---

[9] *Cours,* IV:328, V:6–7, 12–17.
[10] *Ibid.,* V:570.
[11] "Plan of the Scientific Operations," IV:572.

ated by a preliminary "philosophic observation." This conclusion is strikingly borne out by his own testimony. In the *Positive Philosophy,* Comte had admittedly presented only a sketch of the historical process, the details and proofs of which were to appear later. When he undertook, however, to put his philosophy of history into definitive shape in the *Positive Polity,* he was obliged to confess that it contained even less historical information and that his readers must turn back to the *Positive Philosophy* for the supporting data. Comte was content, as he put it, with "coördinated assertions" of his historical generalizations, "leaving the verification and development of them to the public."[12]

This evidence suggests that Comte's historical method is hardly distinguishable from traditional procedures involved in the construction of a philosophy of history. Although he sensed quite clearly that the comparative method and the method of deducing social process from laws of human nature failed to settle the vital question of what any actual historical succession had been, Comte never found a satisfactory solution to the problem.

Use of the comparative method involved acceptance of some principle on which culture differences in space could be arranged in a presumably temporal series. Comte and his contemporaries had no real doubts that the correct principle lay in the view that change was natural, inevitable, progressive, parallel among distinct societies, from the simple to the complex, and, more specifically, from a condition unlike that represented by modern Western Europe to a condition like it. He was also convinced that change, so far as it was natural, was slow and gradual and proceeded from the nature of man himself, uninfluenced by extraneous elements.

It is evident that these ideas in themselves constitute an elaborate philosophy of history, and it is not surprising, therefore, that Comte's historical method, operating through "philosophic observation of the past," should have yielded precisely that set of assumptions necessary to an application of the comparative method. His rejection of empirical-historical investigation as inappropriate to an abstract science of society left him with the comparative method and all its inadequacies, which Comte himself recognized.

HERBERT SPENCER (1820–1903)

Like Comte, Herbert Spencer was a strong advocate of a historical science of society, and saw scientific history as something quite different from the study ordinarily pursued by traditional historians. They, ac-

---

[12] *System of Positive Polity,* III:xi.

cording to Spencer, had been concerned only with a narration of *events*, with "the doings of kings, court-intrigues, international quarrels, victories and defeats, concerning all of which no definite forecasts are possible." They were devoted to the individual, the transitory, or the exceptional, and such materials, he maintained, are simply "unorganizable" as a basis for scientific propositions. Because they were not dealing with a scientific subject matter, historians were accordingly reduced to seeking causal explanations in terms of the motives of great men or the intercession of Providence.[13]

Sociology was to be a radically different sort of history. Although it must deal with man's past and with questions of coming-to-be, it could do so only by attending to that class of phenomena admitting of scientific coördination. The facts must be grasped in their ensemble in order to trace the consensus of coexisting social phenomena as well as the "corresponding delineations of succeeding ages." The highest office of the historian, in Spencer's view, was to furnish the materials on which sociologists would work for the determination of ultimate laws of social phenomena.

The resulting account of the human past was referred to by Spencer as a "natural history of society" in which change is depicted as "growth" consequent upon natural causes. Like geology or biology, sociology would describe the structure, functions, and development of a certain kind of entity. Society had a "nature," and evolution was a result of that nature. A principal task of sociology was to derive the history of society from an analysis of the nature of society.[14]

In seeking means of carrying out this analysis, Spencer adopted the analogy between society and an organism. He made it quite clear that his use of biological terms in describing society was not just a matter of metaphor; these terms were expressive of a "fact."[15] When he discovered von Baer's observation that animals and plants develop from the homogeneous to the heterogeneous, therefore, Spencer was prepared to accept this generalization as equally applicable to the social organism, and he was thus led directly to his theory of social evolution. It described "the history of all organisms whatever."[16]

---

[13] For Spencer's critique of traditional historiography, see his *Autobiography* (London, 1904), II:184, 253, 264–265, 352; "What Knowledge is of Most Worth?" in his *Education: Intellectual, Moral, and Physical* (New York, 1908), pp. 51–54; *The Study of Sociology* (New York, 1874), pp. 11, 25–44, 70–71, 386; "Perverted History," in his *Facts and Comments* (New York, 1902), p. 279. Cf. J. M. Robertson, *A History of Freethought in the Nineteenth Century* (New York, 1930), II:339.

[14] Herbert Spencer, "The Social Organism," in his *Essays: Scientific, Political, and Speculative* (New York, 1899–1904), I:266; *An Autobiography*, II:107.

[15] *Study of Sociology*, p. 330.

[16] *An Autobiography*, I:384–385, 551, II:486; "Progress, its Law and Cause," in *Essays*, I:10.

Having provided himself with a general notion of what the evolution of society had been, Spencer was now ready to make full application of what Comte had called the comparative method. He felt justified in saying that we know the tendency of man has been toward greater heterogeneity because we know civilized man (i.e., Western European man) is more heterogeneous than the Australian aborigine. Society presents itself in its "first and lowest" form, a homogeneous mass of individuals, in "existing" savage tribes. The gradual differentiation of society can be traced up through other communities on a slightly higher level and the series continued by reference to the extinct civilizations of Assyria, Egypt, "the East," Greece, and Rome. The most recent condition is represented by Europeans.[17]

Spencer, unlike Comte, was not troubled by the fact that this procedure yielded only a coexistent series. He was apparently undisturbed by the circumstance that Western European and Australian aborigine both existed in the present and that if the latter's society was to be placed "before" the former in a temporal series, that arrangement called for justification. Spencer's contempt for historical detail prevented his ever seeking to derive from such material, even by "philosophic observation," a general view of what the temporal succession or consecutive series might have been. His synthesis of the past, his basic theory of change, his principle of arrangement for the handling of ethnographic data rested entirely, in terms of his own system, on the biological analogy.

In preparing his great treatise on sociology, therefore, Spencer found no occasion to ponder the kind of materials he would use or what he would do with them. He and his associates examined "some books of travel" and gathered general information on different societies. The "differences" Spencer encountered were simply "stages of evolution," which, when arranged in accord with an elaboration of the homogeneous-heterogeneous principle, presumably represented man's history.[18]

Although Spencer saw no need for testing his evolutionary sequence with direct evidence of actual historical succession, he was nevertheless aware of the dangers involved in the assumption of unilinear social progress. He noted that societies did not differ merely in their stages of growth and that they were not simply variations on a single type or species. Social change had been divergent and redivergent and had been affected by such "intrusions" as invasions, minglings of peoples,

---

[17] "Progress, its Law and Cause," I:15, 17, 19–35.

[18] Herbert Spencer, *Descriptive Sociology; or Groups of Sociological Facts, Classified and Arranged* (London, 1873), Division III, No. 1, Part 1-C, "Provisional Preface," pp. iii–iv; *An Autobiography*, pp. 172–173, note 261.

and the annexation or loss of territory. These circumstances, Spencer admitted, were bound to obscure the results of comparison. There is no evidence, however, that an awareness of such difficulties seriously modified Spencer's procedure. He insisted on regarding intrusions as exceptional or as discontinuities in the "normal processes" of social growth. Hence they did not constitute for him a subject to be investigated, and he was content to draw those "general conclusions" derivable from the use of the comparative method.[19]

Spencer's investigation of the relations of coexistence and sequence among different social phenomena can in no sense be regarded simply as a procedure for reaching a social morphology. The result was not merely a convenient arrangement of items for a file or a museum. The criteria on which the arrangement was based were, after all, derived from a theory of change, and the series is supposed to depict a process in time—a history in Spencer's sense of the term. Certain generalizations, he observed, emerge from the classification. Foremost among these is the assertion that "in this order has social evolution gone on, and only in this order does it appear to be possible." Societies, he added, "arise in the order shown," and the "stages of compounding and re-compounding have to be passed through in succession."[20] There can be no doubt that Spencer felt he was writing human history—a generalized account, to be sure, but nevertheless one that contained those elements essential to his conception of a scientific demonstration.

JOHN STUART MILL (1806–1875)

English logicians in the nineteenth century displayed a lively interest in the possibility of scientific historical study. An earlier conviction that the way to a "natural history" of man lay through an introspective analysis of human nature itself had apparently fallen into disrepute, and new, more strictly historical, approaches were being sought.[21] The comparative or historical method came to be regarded as a promising alternative.

Thus we find Thomas Fowler endorsing the "historical method" (an

---

[19] Herbert Spencer, *Principles of Sociology* (New York, 1910), II:242–243, III:331; *Study of Sociology*, p. 329.

[20] *Principles of Sociology*, I:555–556. Cf. Morris Ginsberg, "Preface" to J. Rumney's *Herbert Spencer's Sociology* (London, 1934), p. 6. Ginsberg's suggestion that Spencer verified inductions arrived at through the comparative method by showing that they followed deductively from the general law of evolution and laws of psychology is difficult to follow. Spencer's law of evolution and his propositions regarding human nature provided him with the principle of arrangement necessary to an application of the comparative method. These "laws" could hardly, therefore, be used to verify results yielded by the comparative method.

[21] See Mill's remarks on Bentham and his school in *Auguste Comte and Positivism*, 2d ed., rev. (London, 1866), p. 84.

application of what he called the method of concomitant variations and what Whewell referred to as the method of gradation) as "specifically applicable to those sciences which deal with man as a progressive being."[22] H. W. B. Joseph regarded the "historical or comparative" method as having revolutionized inquiry into the history of social institutions, and he anticipated the achievement of fruitful results from a comparison of "institutions of widely different ages, or of peoples who though contemporaneous stand at widely different levels of civilization and of thought."[23]

But it is John Stuart Mill who deserves greatest credit for placing upon Comte's methodology the stamp of full logical approval. This activity of Mill on behalf of Positivism resulted in its fairly widespread acceptance in England and its reimportation into France with the added weight of scholarly endorsement.[24]

Mill shared Comte's and Spencer's conviction that sociology must deal with questions of temporal succession, and he also agreed that traditional procedures in the study of history were inappropriate to a scientific handling of the problem. He felt that most of those who had speculated on the general characteristics of history had subjected them to certain "twists and exaggerations." Some allotted too much and others too little influence to the effects of accidents in history, while still others misconstrued the influence of individuals. Mill praised Comte for having avoided the "vulgar mistake of supposing that the course of history has no tendencies of its own" and agreed with him that the real stuff of history did not lie in small causes or the acts of kings, conquerors, and founders of philosophies. He was convinced that Positivism followed a true middle course in these matters, and he advised anyone who "disbelieves that the philosophy of history can be made a science" to reserve judgment until he had read the works of Auguste Comte.[25]

The major problem of social science, according to Mill, is to determine "what are the causes which produce, and the phenomena which characterize, States of Society generally." States of society display certain "uniformities of coexistence"; i.e., the various elements in society stand in definite relationships, so that given the status of one element

---

[22] Thomas Fowler, *The Elements of Inductive Logic*, 6th ed., rev. (Oxford, 1894), pp. 204–205.
[23] H. W. B. Joseph, *An Introduction to Logic* (Oxford, 1906), p. 522.
[24] John Theodore Merz, *A History of European Thought in the Nineteenth Century* (London, 1907–1914), I:18–19. It is not implied, of course, that Spencer was indebted to Mill in this respect. Ideas involved in the comparative-historical method were common to educated nineteenth-century Englishmen. Mill offered little more than a systematic reiteration of old ideas on this point.
[25] *Auguste Comte and Positivism*, pp. 106, 113–114.

we can expect to find all other elements occupying a corresponding status. Societies, in short, are like whole organisms. But, Mill argued, these uniformities of coexistence are a product of the way in which society comes to be, and thus the most important problem of social science is a historical problem. We must, he wrote, "find the laws according to which any state of society produces the state which succeeds it and takes its place." For Mill this meant that we must come to grips with the "great and vexed question" of progress—"an idea involved in every just conception of social phenomena as the subject of science." The question did not delay Mill, however, for he was confident that the idea of progress was a proper conception of social change and, therefore, of human history.[26] Acceptance of this "idea of a trajectory or progress" provided Mill, of course, with the requisites to an application of the comparative method.

Mill had read his Positivism carefully, however, and there was a feature of it that appealed strongly to his empirical bent. This was Comte's insistence that any judgment concerning the course of social development must rest, finally, on an examination of what the actual historical succession had been. Mill took a further step and contended that a first operation in the comparative or historical method must involve turning to the "facts of history."[27] The result of such an investigation would presumably be a body of empirical generalizations descriptive of the way in which "any state of society produces the state which succeeds it."

As with Comte, however, we find that Mill failed to discuss just how the empirical-historical inquiry was to be conducted. He described this part of the new science of man merely as "a study and analysis of the general facts of history," according to the method "now generally adopted by the most advanced thinkers on the Continent."[28] If this reference is to Comte's "philosophic observation of the past," the historical method still remains obscure, and Mill has again evaded the crucial question of the specific means to be employed in handling what he and his contemporaries designated as the central problem of social science.

This is a harsh appraisal of Mill's efforts, but its justness is confirmed when we consider that his proposed method led him to advise social scientists to seek their historical generalizations in the observation of only a "few instances." The reason given for this curious limitation was that few nations had ever attained a high stage of social progress, and fewer still as a result of independent development.[29] Clearly, then,

---

[26] J. S. Mill, *A System of Logic* (London, 1900), VI:x, 1–3.
[27] *Auguste Comte and Positivism*, p. 85.
[28] *System of Logic*, VI:x, 3.
[29] *Ibid.*, VI:x, 4.

Mill was not actually seeking a method that would explain how any state of society produces the state which succeeds it, but was interested rather in means of demonstrating a progressive movement in history. It was this that focused his attention on a few nations (in Western Europe) which he chose to regard as having reached a high stage of development. He was justified, within the presuppositions of the historical or comparative method, in centering his inquiry there, for then all other peoples or nations became the approximate equivalents of earlier historical phases of social development in Europe.

CONCLUSION

Nineteenth-century sociology began, avowedly, as a historical science of society. Its advocates insisted that social order and functions could be understood and social reform accomplished only through grappling with the more fundamental problem of social change. This problem was, in the largest sense of the term, a historical problem.

In describing either this problem or their method of attacking it as "historical," however, it must be recognized that Comte, Spencer, and Mill used the term in a sense radically different from that of the traditional historian. Whereas the historian undertook to produce faithful representations of detailed, concrete, time-and-place events in the experiences of particular peoples, it was precisely this kind of specific, chronological data that the sociologists rejected as unorganizable or unamenable to scientific treatment. Such data, according to Comte and Spencer, were unique, and therefore not to be embraced by any generalizing scientific law. This curious conviction that there is in the record of human experience a class of particulars about which we cannot generalize calls for some explanation. One purpose of the second part of this study will be to seek an explanation in the fund of basic ideas inherited by nineteenth-century students.

It is instructive to notice that the strength of this assumption concerning the uniqueness of historical events was such that Comte and Mill (and, to a lesser extent, Spencer) continued to accept it even though they clearly recognized that the construction of a developmental or evolutionary sequence of social forms demanded some kind of empirical inquiry into the "facts" of history. There is thus little point in arguing that the failure of these men to arrive at valid historical generalizations was due to their use of what is now regarded as an inadequate "comparative method." They saw the weaknesses of that method; Comte, in fact, presented a more telling critique of it than has appeared in most recent discussions. They were forced to rely on the comparative method because they had denied themselves access to empirical-historical materials.

What the so-called historical method yielded was actually a philosophy of history that was identical with the set of assumptions used to arrange social or cultural differences in a presumed temporal and developmental series under the comparative method.[30] This philosophy or "general view" of history pictured society as in a perpetual state of flux. Social change was broadly described as natural, continuous, slow, gradual, and progressive. The movement was from the simple to the complex, and "simple" was identified with the non-European, "complex" with the European. In elaborated form, this picture of change provided the criteria used to construct a "consecutive series" from a "coexistent series."

Use of the comparative method demanded particular emphasis on the gradualness of change, for the method offered no means of accounting for discontinuities in the ideal series. The close relation between a theory of gradual change, which tends to discount the significance of events in a continuous process, and the assumption that historical events are unique suggests their possible common derivation from a broader complex of ideas. This question will be explored in Part II.

Finally, the quite uncritical acceptance by nineteenth-century sociologists of that comprehensive theory of social change commonly called the "idea of progress," suggests the existence of an intellectual heritage of which they were not fully aware. The content of that particular heritage and its implications for the task sociologists set themselves will also be examined in Part II.

---

[30] It is perhaps this circumstance that accounts for the common expression, "comparative *or* historical method." It also explains the comment of some historians (e.g., J. M. Robertson, *op. cit.*, II:343) that the method yielded only a comparative anatomy of social forms and not a process in any sense of the term.

CHAPTER II

THE AIMS OF ANTHROPOLOGY

WHEN, AT THE BEGINNING of the twentieth century, Frederic William Maitland observed that "by and by anthropology will have the choice between being history and being nothing," he was protesting against an evolutionist approach that had characterized the study of culture in the preceding half century. Granting the justice of his criticism, it must be noted that even the most extreme nineteenth-century evolutionist was deeply concerned with a study of the human or cultural past and had, indeed, claimed to follow a method for studying "history" that was superior to procedures followed by the academic historian.

Thus an early historian of anthropology pointed out in 1863 that the study had as its most important objective "what is more generally known as the science of history." It was to be a certain kind of history, true,—one that would explain how men "must needs act" in order to produce the regular sequence of events known as "history." But this activity would still deserve the name of history, for even the ordinary historian presumed some common principle of action among men in order to construct his narrative. What anthropologists proposed to do was "explain how those common principles have operated from the origin of man, and produced all past and present history."[1]

EDWARD BURNETT TYLOR (1832–1917)

Tylor adopted just this point of view in his great pioneering work in anthropology. He noted, as had Comte and Spencer, that there was a general reluctance to proceed along scientific lines in the study of history. Academic historians, misled by "notions of arbitrary impulses, causeless freaks, chance and nonsense and indefinite unaccountability," had contented themselves with particularized accounts of the lives of tribes and nations that could never rise to the level of scientific principle. Tylor proposed to circumvent these limitations by making culture the subject of historical investigation.[2]

Since he was convinced that the object of a historical study of culture was to explain the present state of things, and because he felt that this must be sought in the condition of "rude and early tribes" as well as in direct historical information about the more "advanced races," Tylor was immediately faced with the question of how the early history of

---

[1] T. Bendyshe, "The History of Anthropology," in *Memoirs Read before the Anthropological Society of London 1863–1864* (London, 1865), pp. 335–336.

[2] Edward Burnett Tylor, *Primitive Culture*, 2d ed. (New York, 1873), I:2, 5, 19.

culture could be recovered in the absence of written historical records. He suggested first that many institutions might be explained, without the aid of history in the usual sense, as "direct products of the human mind." But he was not satisfied with this procedure as applied to the greater part of culture. Most cultural phenomena, he believed, had been shaped from a "complication of events," and this circumstance called for a "laborious piecing together of their previous history." Hence, he advocated recourse to indirect evidence in such areas as antiquities, language, and mythology as a second and more reliable technique. Specifically, this involved a comparison of similarities among various cultures as a means of demonstrating some historical connection between the peoples concerned.[3]

Although Tylor's aim was to get information about the past, this way of stating the problem involved him in quite puzzling questions as to the significance of cultural similarities. Even granting that there was a substantial similarity of customs, arts, and ideas among the "lower tribes," Tylor found it difficult to tell whether any particular similarity had arisen as a result of the "like working of men's minds under like conditions" or as a result of blood relationship or contact between the peoples displaying the similarity. In later controversy over this problem it is often forgotten that a consideration of these alternatives was originally important to Tylor only because in the former case similarities were of no value for reconstructing history, while in the latter, he felt, they had a very high value.[4]

Not only did Tylor fail to solve this problem even to his own satisfaction, but, as his work proceeded, his strictly historical orientation gave way to an interest in the "unity of nature" and the "fixity of its laws." A search for evidence of historical connections that might unravel the "complication of events" that had produced the present was supplanted by preoccupation with the construction of a "philosophy of primeval history." His avowed purpose now was to establish the thesis that the present savage state represented an early condition out of which higher culture had gradually evolved in a progressive manner.[5]

An acceptance of contemporary savagery as representative of an early condition of mankind in general involved the assumption of a certain temporal sequence in culture history. Savagery and civilization were, as Comte had noted, temporally coexistent, and before they could be placed in a consecutive series historical evidence must justify the

---

[3] Tylor, *Researches into the Early History of Mankind and the Development of Civilization*, 3d ed. (New York, 1878), pp. 1–4, 275.
[4] *Researches*, pp. 5, 53, 87, 169, 204, 373, *et passim*.
[5] *Primitive Culture*, I:2, 25, 32.

arrangement. Tylor was obviously aware of this, for he did argue that direct historical evidence of later civilizational development supported the progressive view of history. But he made no historical study of the presumed development, trusting rather to "general knowledge" and the "long experience" of ethnologists for support of the proposition that an arrangement of cultures in a progressive series probably represented "their actual sequence in history."[6]

Tylor, of course, did not leave the matter here. "General knowledge" of history seemed to suggest that civilization had grown out of savagery, but he looked elsewhere for supporting evidence. He claimed to find it in the "survival" of savagery in civilization. If, Tylor felt, remnants or relics of contemporary savage customs, rituals, or ideas could be found in contemporary civilization, this would suggest that the latter had evolved out of the former. A prodigious amount of work went into the search for similar traits in savage and civilized societies. Tylor's failure to realize that the identification of a survival as such depended upon the assumption of the very developmentalism that he had set out to validate has been subjected to criticism elsewhere.[7] The doctrine of survivals offered no fruitful way around the "complication of events" that Tylor had earlier recognized as the empirical matrix within which historical process must be sought.

Anthropologists are, of course, indebted to Tylor in many respects, and even with regard to the questions treated here he performed a service in calling attention to problems that the comparative method raised and did not solve. If he finally adopted this procedure for historical study, he did so with some awareness of the difficulties involved. No such generous judgment is due the majority of Tylor's contemporaries and immediate successors.

LEWIS HENRY MORGAN (1818–1881)

For Lewis Henry Morgan the comparative method was simply the method of anthropology, and the assumption that the general course of cultural change was already known was never questioned by him. "Convincing evidence," he believed, proved that savagery preceded barbarism, and barbarism preceded civilization in "all the tribes of mankind." Progress had been realized by "slow, almost imperceptible steps," it was both "natural" and "necessary," and it was to be accepted as "historically true" of all humanity. To Morgan it was simply a fact that "higher" and "lower" were synonyms, respectively, for "later" and

---

[6] *Ibid.*, I:14–15, 26–27, 37, 63–64.

[7] See Margaret T. Hodgen, *The Doctrine of Survivals* (London, 1936), Chapter 5 and sources cited there.

"earlier." Male and female classes were older than the gentes because the gentile organization was higher; the gens as it "now" exists among American Indians was its earliest historical form; and so on.[8]

As later supporters of Morgan have noted, he did not ignore the facts of contact and borrowing or diffusion among peoples. This observation, however, did not lead him either to a historical investigation of such occurrences or to their use as indirect evidence of historical processes. Nor did an acknowledgment of diffusion interfere with Morgan's conception of parallel developmental series for each people. All tribes, he noted, had shared in each other's inventions and discoveries where a continental connection existed, "but the inferior tribes must have appreciated their value before they could appropriate them." Borrowing, therefore, did not disrupt the normal series, and it was permissible to ignore, as Morgan customarily did, specific historical evidence of diffusion and deal with development as a direct product of human nature. As Morgan put it, the human mind is the same in all individuals, tribes, and nations, and so it *must* work in the same channels to produce in separated regions and separated ages "a logically connected chain of common experiences." The evolution of culture from lower to higher forms was thus to be conceived as a process of the "logical operations of the human mind working in uniform but predetermined channels." Progress was to be investigated not as a result of historical events of diffusion or borrowing, but as a consequence of the "improvable mental and moral qualities which belong to the human species."[9]

JOHN FERGUSON McLENNAN (1827–1881)

Failure to seek historical evidence in an attack upon a clearly historical problem is even more strikingly apparent in the work of McLennan. Firm in the belief that the significant early history of culture could not be compiled from ordinary documents, and making the usual judgment that origins must be recovered, McLennan also saw his task as that of discovering "what the early history of mankind *must have been.*"[10] He turned, with no hesitation, to the comparative method as a proper means to this end. The assumptions necessary to the use of this procedure did not deter him. He simply noted that the "great diversity of phases of civilization" revealed by the voyage literature "readily suggests" that the more advanced peoples had passed through a condition exhibited by

---

[8] Lewis H. Morgan, *Ancient Society* (Chicago, 1877), pp. v–vii, 3, 48, 64, *et passim.*
[9] *Ibid.*, pp. 8, 39, 262, 273, 390, 455.
[10] John Ferguson McLennan, *Studies in Ancient History, Second Series, Comprising an Inquiry into the Origin of Exogamy*, ed. by Eleonora A. McLennan and Arthur Platt (London, 1896), p. 7. (Italics added.)

the less advanced, while ancient historical nations represented an intermediate stage of development.[11]

McLennan proposed to confirm in detail this obvious order of succession by finding a persistence of lower cultural forms in higher stages. A carry-over of symbols from the lower to the higher form was evidence, he felt, both for recovery of the earlier form and connection of the later with it. The procedure is similar to Tylor's, and it obviously rested on a determination of the original form. As McLennan himself observed, we can recognize a symbol when we see one only through our acquaintance with "the rude modes of life with which the examination of the lower races makes us familiar."[12] Without his developmentalist assumptions, McLennan's symbols obviously could not be identified; the symbols could not, therefore, be used to support those assumptions.

The feature of McLennan's work, however, that is of chief interest to the present discussion is his assertion at one point that he was not concerned with a temporal problem at all. He sought to infer, he tells us, the "historical order" in which certain cultural forms arose. The first step in this task was to describe the least developed races as they existed in the present. These were the "lowest and simplest" peoples, and they represented "origins," "germal" forms, or the "most ancient condition of man." But "old" here did not mean old in chronology, McLennan asserted; it meant old in structure. Thus, the culture that is most ancient is the one "which lies nearest the beginning of human progress considered as a development, and that is most modern which is farthest removed from it."[13]

Although it is quite clear from the body of his work that McLennan was actually interested in settling questions of temporal succession, these reservations reveal in interesting fashion his recognition of the fact that he presented no satisfactory procedure for doing so. As a result, he sought to abdicate from the position of historian entirely and defend the operation of constructing merely a classification of cultures based on criteria that had no temporal significance whatever. The abstract quality of historical science on which Comte insisted here reaches a point where even time itself is omitted.

THE "HISTORICAL" STUDY OF INSTITUTIONS

The repeated claim that nineteenth-century social scientists, presumably in response to Darwin's influence, emphasized a historical approach to the study of society and culture calls for qualification. The literature

[11] *Ibid.*, pp. 8–10.
[12] *Ibid.*, pp. 17, 21.
[13] *Ibid.*, pp. 16–19.

that followed immediately upon the so-called pioneer work of Tylor, Morgan, and McLennan is marked by an eager acceptance of the comparative method, an intense concern with origins, and a common endeavor to construct stages in a developmental cultural series. But there is little evidence of the kind of historical study that would seek to explore Comte's "actual" succession, cope with Mill's "facts" of history, or unravel Tylor's "complication of events."

Armed with the assumptions of evolutionism and seemingly strengthened by the concept of survivals and the greater accuracy and detail of ethnographic data, scholars in every field of humanistic inquiry set themselves the tasks of discovering origins and tracing the serial development of every conceivable form of social institution. The cautious procedure of Tylor as historian was forgotten in an ambitious and enthusiastic effort to uncover "absolute" origins in the human mind and to derive evolutionary sequences by psychogenetic methods.

Thus Andrew Lang praised Tylor for having avoided the pitfalls of degenerationism that had caused a temporary diversion from the ideas of Lucretius and for having returned finally to the "half forgotten sense of Fontenelle" that enabled one to see mythology as a natural product of the mental condition of savages. The question of method was settled for Lang. Evolution was a fact, and all that remained for scholars was a more detailed investigation of a process whose main outlines were already known. The comparative method, and especially the doctrine of survivals, were accepted as the key that opened the old lock of ancient Greek myth and, in a larger sense, revealed the slow evolution of Western European culture out of savagery.[14]

A similar confidence marked Letourneau's investigation of the origin and development of property. The inspiration of his work, he confessed, was drawn from the idea that existing inferior races are living representatives of our primitive ancestors. Letourneau, in 1892, could see no reason for questioning the propriety of the comparative method: it was "the very basis of evolutionary sociology." The whole problem of checking a particular arrangement of the coexistent with some empirical examination of the historically consecutive forms of property was simply ignored.[15]

For all his prodigious learning and industry, Sir James George Frazer stands out in the present connection as a caricature of the

[14] Andrew Lang, "Edward Burnett Tylor," in *Anthropological Essays Presented to Edward Burnett Tylor in Honour of his 75th Birthday, Oct. 2, 1907* (London, 1907); *Modern Mythology* (London, 1897), pp. 6–7.

[15] Ch. Letourneau, *Property: Its Origin and Development* (London, 1892), see esp. pp. ix, 364–365, 369–371.

methodological absentmindedness of his time. For him, social anthropology rested squarely on the assumption that "civilization has always and everywhere been evolved out of savagery," and if anyone disputed the point Frazer did "not think it worthwhile to argue with him."[16] He was content to assume the similarity of the human mind throughout time and space and to derive from this the conclusion that since the most "backward" races practice magic without religion, the "civilized" races must have passed through a similar phase. Discovery of survivals of magic in civilization confirmed the hypothesis.[17]

The relation between the biological analogy and the comparative method is as evident in Frazer's case as it was in Comte's or Spencer's. The study of social anthropology could, Frazer argued in a classic passage, be regarded as "the embryology of human thought and institutions." Savage man represented a retarded stage of social development, so that his customs and beliefs were evidence of the evolution of the human mind in the same way that the embryo was evidence of the evolution of the human body. In larger perspective, savage society in its "various stages of evolution" shows us the early path that civilization "must have travelled" in its upward progress.[18] With evidence such as this at hand it was unnecessary for Frazer to be concerned with actual historical succession.

Frazer's extreme position did not, however, set him apart from his fellow investigators. While he sought the origin of religion in savage ideas, Marett was searching, by the same method, for its beginnings in savage emotions. In another field, Harrison had been inspired by the revelation that "modern science" had provided means for revealing the early history of art. The new method was to use savage materials and survivals of the primitive among European peasants. Gummere, after seriously questioning some features of the comparative method, proceeded to use it for sketching the origins of poetry. Veblen caused a stir among professional economists at the close of the century by using savages and survivals to recover the "origin and line of derivation" of the leisure class as an economic factor in the present. Dealey, in 1909, followed a pattern common among students of government when he employed the method to trace the origin and development of the state, which he regarded as "practically uniform" wherever it took place. And in 1927 Briffault searched out the origins of sentiments and institu-

---

[16] James George Frazer, *Psyche's Task*, 2d ed. (London, 1913), p. 162.
[17] Frazer, *The Golden Bough: A Study in Magic and Religion,* abridged ed. (New York, 1922), pp. 2, 301–302, 385–386, 479–480, *et passim.*
[18] *Psyche's Task,* pp. 162–163, 171.

tions in a collection of savage customs and modern survivals that rivaled in bulk the work of Frazer himself.[19]

Throughout these and many similar discussions[20] the problem of cultural similarities persisted, but an interest in similarities as clues to historical connection—Tylor's original concern—came more and more to be replaced by a preoccupation with cultural likeness as a confirmation of developmental assumptions of uniformity or parallelism. Attention was consequently diverted from a quest for historical evidence bearing on the circumstances of cultural changes. Tylor was criticized for placing so much emphasis on diffusion and borrowing, and it was forgotten that his original purpose had been to examine these phenomena as evidence bearing on the history of culture rather than as mere explanations of similarities.[21] W. D. Wallis' later observation that conclusions with regard to independent invention or borrowing could not be reached through an analysis of similarities "where there is absence of historical proof" indicates the extent to which the ambition of anthropologists to pursue a historical science of man had been lost sight of amidst debate on other problems.[22]

Issues raised by evolutionist assumptions, the comparative method, and the uses to which survivals might legitimately be put were debated

---

[19] R. R. Marett, *The Threshold of Religion*, 2d ed. (London, 1914); Jane Ellen Harrison, *Ancient Art and Ritual* (New York, 1913), see esp. pp. 23–24; F. B. Gummere, *Beginnings of Poetry* (New York, 1901); Thorstein Veblen, *The Theory of the Leisure Class* (New York, 1919 [1899]); see also his *Instinct of Workmanship* (New York, 1914) and "The Beginnings of Ownership," *American Journal of Sociology*, 4(1898):352–365; James Quayle Dealey, *The Development of the State* (New York, 1909); Robert Briffault, *The Mothers: A Study of the Origins of Sentiments and Institutions*, 3 vols. (New York, 1927).

[20] Examples of evolutionism and the use of the comparative method in this period are legion. For a sample of some of the briefer statements see: A. Lane-Fox Pitt-Rivers, *The Evolution of Culture and other Essays*, ed. by J. L. Myres (Oxford, 1906); Daniel G. Brinton, "The Aims of Anthropology," in *Proceedings of the American Association for the Advancement of Science, 44th Meeting, 1895* (Salem, 1896), pp. 1–17; George F. Moore, "The History of Religions in the Nineteenth Century," in *Congress of Arts and Sciences, St. Louis, 1904* (Boston, 1906), II:432–442; Carl D. Buck, "The Relations of Comparative Grammar to other Branches of Learning," *ibid.*, III:32–52; A. C. Haddon, "Ethnology: Its Scope and Problems," *ibid.*, V:549–570; F. B. Jevons, "Graeco-Italian Magic," in *Anthropology and the Classics*, ed. by R. R. Marett (Oxford, 1908), pp. 93–120; J. Dorsey Forrest, *The Development of Western Civilization* (Chicago, 1907), see esp. pp. 377–390; Paul Caullet, *Éléments de Sociologie* (Paris, 1913); Paul Vinogradoff and Hugh Goitein, "Comparative Jurisprudence," *Encyclopaedia Britannica*, 14th ed., 13:200–206.

[21] See Andrew Lang, "Edward Burnett Tylor," p. 3.

[22] W. D. Wallis, "Similarities in Culture," *American Anthropologist*, 19(1917): 51–52. For other discussions of the problem of similarities see: O. T. Mason, "Similarities in Culture," *American Anthropologist*, 8(1895):101–117; Henry Balfour, "Introduction," to A. Lane-Fox Pitt-Rivers, *op. cit.*, Paul Ehrenreich, "Zur Frage der Beurtheilung und Bewerthung Ethnographischer Analogien," *Correspondenz-Blatt der Deutschen Gesellschaft fur Anthropologie, Ethnologie, und Urgeschichte*, 34(1903):176–180.

throughout the later nineteenth and early twentieth centuries with regard to other questions besides the significance of cultural similarities. Did the savage really represent original, primeval man or a subsequent development? Which particular savage tribe or people represented the lowest, and hence earliest, state of culture? Could absolute origins be discovered in human nature, and, if so, should they be sought in individual or group psychology, in primitive intellect or primitive emotion? Just how were the successive "stages" of evolution to be arranged, and on the basis of what criteria? Could specific examples of a trait or institution properly be isolated from their cultural and social context and arranged as museum pieces to depict an abstract evolution of the considered item? Was the evolution of material culture, or of any other single aspect of culture, a sufficient index to general cultural evolution, or was the notion of the simultaneous development of cultural elements unreliable?

It must be acknowledged that attention to problems such as these led anthropologists to promising new perspectives. Functionalist theory, for example, was formulated largely in response to serious doubts concerning the evolutionist synthesis. But here again the initial objective of historical reconstruction was neglected in attacking or defending propositions relative to the use of the comparative method. As it became apparent that historical processes could not be depicted in the absence of historical evidence, anthropologists tended to postpone or abandon the enterprise and devote themselves to other tasks. A historical science of man was relinquished as an aim because particular means for attaining it were judged inadequate.

Conclusion

Like the sociologists, anthropologists in the second half of the nineteenth century resolved to pursue a scientific history of man. Their point of departure in this enterprise was a rejection of both the procedures and the materials utilized by traditional historians. This rejection of concrete time-and-place data—events in the histories of "tribes and nations"—was accompanied at the outset by an effort to derive historical evidence indirectly from a classification of cultural similarities. When apparently irresolvable issues arose to block this operation there was a return to evolutionist or developmental assumptions that provided an answer to the historical question. The idea of progress was accepted as a philosophy of history, and anthropologists busied themselves with a mere arrangement of cultural differences to form a presumably temporal series in accord with the criteria so furnished. When the rather obvious shortcomings of this procedure were recognized a reaction against the entire historical enterprise resulted in a pursuit of other problems.

The argument that anthropologists became involved in these difficulties because they were dealing with nonliterate and therefore history-less peoples is not altogether convincing. Their original aim was a science of man—everywhere, at all times, in all his manifestations—and this has apparently been a continuing objective. Whatever other considerations led to a primary concern with nonliterate peoples, one obviously was the conviction that such peoples furnished a clue to the early history of culture. In undertaking first to explore the more remote reaches of historical experience anthropologists might well have been confronted with the problems that commonly plague the historian who investigates periods for which evidence is scant. But these problems are of a quite different order from those associated with the assumption that contemporary nonliterate tribes represent the past or that present cultural differences, when properly arranged, depict cultural evolution through time.

Given an express interest in history, anthropologists nevertheless refrained from using available historical data for any period, remote or recent. Faced with the persistent problem of how men have come to be as they are, culturally different, they accepted instead an elaborate philosophy of culture history that provided *a priori* answers to the questions posed by the "complication of events" in human experience. The historical science of culture failed, then; but why? An answer to this question is to be sought not so much in an analysis of the comparative method or evolutionist assumptions as in the basic perspectives that nineteenth-century scholars inherited from a tradition deeply rooted in Western thought.

CHAPTER III

REACTIONS TO THE PROPOSED SCIENCE OF HISTORY

THE HISTORIAN'S RESPONSE

THE EFFORTS of nineteenth-century sociologists and anthropologists to construct a "true" or "scientific" history of society or culture might be supposed to have attracted the attention of traditional historians and to have raised issues of fundamental importance in the study of man. The historian's profession had long been held in highest repute, he enjoyed a secure and dignified position in the humanities, and his method of narrative presentation had, since the time of Herodotus, been accepted as the proper means of recounting the temporal experiences of mankind. Men looked to written history as "the witness of ages, the light of truth, the life of memory, the herald of antiquity, the champion of virtue, and the avenger of vice."[1] Academic historians who had accepted and sought to meet the heavy responsibilities of their calling could well have been disturbed at being relegated, at best, to the role of handmaid in a sociological or anthropological science. Comte had branded their work as a species of barren empiricism. Spencer had accused them of perverting the record. Tylor had reproached them for their failure to proceed along scientific lines. And in 1895 Brinton predicted: "The time will come, and that soon, when sound historians will adopt as their guide the principles and methods of ethnologic science, because by these alone can they assign to the isolated fact its right place in the vast structure of human development."[2]

Although these critiques and the bold new programs for historical study that accompanied them would seem to have placed the whole historiographic enterprise in jeopardy, there is little evidence of dismay or alarm among historians. Comte and Spencer felt that they were introducing a new science of history, yet when G. P. Gooch reviewed the history and historians of the nineteenth century in 1913 he calmly devoted a single sentence to Comte and refrained altogether from mentioning Spencer. A positive reaction was not, however, entirely absent, and an examination of it will serve to clarify the grounds upon which students of human history on the one hand, and students of

---

[1] Thomas Greenwood, *Introductory Lectures on the Study of History* (London, 1835), pp. 11–12.

[2] Daniel G. Brinton, "The Aims of Anthropology," in *Proceedings of the American Association for the Advancement of Science, 44th Meeting, 1895* (Salem, 1896), p. 7.

social or cultural evolution on the other, came to an understanding that would perpetuate their traditional division of labor.

The first protest against positive or scientific history was made on moral rather than methodological grounds. There was something revolting to many nineteenth-century minds in the idea that history ran a determinate course. It seemed to challenge man's ability to make his own history, and it raised in disturbing forms the question of freedom of will. Hence many of Comte's and Spencer's critics were clergymen and philosophers who debated with great vigor the ethical, religious, and metaphysical issues raised by the positive and synthetic systems.[3]

Goldwin Smith, among historians, challenged Comte on this moral plane. In a series of lectures delivered at Oxford between 1859 and 1861, Smith frankly announced himself as a deeply religious man whose conception of the "pure morality and true religion" placed him in opposition to any deterministic interpretation of human affairs. Man's free will, he maintained, rendered impossible a science of history.[4]

Smith's attack did not, however, hinge on the religious issue alone, for he went on to scrutinize the Comtean position with a relentlessness that few historians then or since have bothered to emulate. He pointed out that the new "science of man" actually violated simple principles of scientific procedure when it set up grand hypotheses incapable of verification. Evidence to test generalizations about human actions must be sought, Smith argued, in the record of human actions. To ignore the individual, as Comte had proposed, was to rule out the only tangible evidence. Speaking as a historian, Smith could not see a "shadow of proof" for the assertion that society began with fetichism and cannibalism or that there had been a succession of theological, metaphysical, and positive stages in intellectual development. That fetichism seemed "lowest" to us was no reason for regarding it as "earliest." Theological and positive intellectual orientations had always gone together; there was really no series here at all.[5]

The strength of Smith's critique lay chiefly in his realization that since Comte's generalizations were not derived from an inspection of historical data their basis must be sought in analogy. He called attention to the danger of bringing physical or biological metaphor into a discussion of history, and in such a way as to make it evident that he did not consider this a question merely of terminology. In plain lan-

---

[3] For an account of some of these disputes see John Watson, *Comte, Mill, and Spencer* (New York, 1895); Charles B. Waite, *Herbert Spencer and his Critics* (Chicago, 1900).

[4] Goldwin Smith, *Lectures on the Study of History* (Toronto, 1873), pp. 44, 48, 79, *et passim*.

[5] *Ibid.*, pp. 48, 56–58, 71–72, 80.

guage he noted that nations simply are not organisms. They are not born, they do not mature, and they do not die like men. Nor are they physical entities. Men do not act in masses; they act in multitudes. To talk about social statics and dynamics does not add to our knowledge of society if society is not a physical body. In short, "development is a word proper to physical organs, which cannot be transferred to the course of a nation without begging the whole question." Smith felt justified in concluding that "the new science of Man is merely a set of terms."[6]

Charles Kingsley, in Spencer's opinion one of the most notorious perverters of history, struck back with arguments similar to Smith's. In an inaugural lecture as Professor of Modern History at the University of Cambridge, Kingsley notified his students that Gibbon would still be the textbook on which they would be examined. "Young sciences," he observed, had produced other works, but these were marked by "wonder, hope, imagination, and . . . passion too, and haste, and bigotry." Those who sought law and order in history had become anesthetized by the limited yield of their scientific fervor.

Dazzled, and that pardonably, by the beauty of the few laws they may have discovered, they are too apt to erect them into gods, and to explain by them all matters in heaven and earth; and apt, too, to patch them where they are weakest, by that most dangerous succedaneum of vague and grand epithets, which very often contain, each of them, an assumption far more important than the law to which they are tacked.[7]

Kingsley did not deny order and progress in history, but he insisted that the laws governing such phenomena were moral rather than mechanical. Historical laws, therefore, must be discovered "not in things, but in persons; in the actions of human beings." The student who grasped the moral dimension of history, who saw the preponderant influence of great men over the masses, and who had developed a keen understanding of human beings was, according to Kingsley, in a much better position to discern law in history than any positive philosopher. Kingsley shuddered at the notion of explaining the crusades "by a hypothesis of overstocked labour-markets on the Continent."[8]

This emphasis on a moral quality in history that rendered scientific considerations inappropriate was echoed by James Anthony Froude. After presenting the usual arguments about free will and the role of the historian as recounter of "what is great and good" and "what is base," Froude proceeded, however, to points that F. H. Bradley en-

---

[6] *Ibid.*, pp. 62, 81.
[7] Charles Kingsley, *The Limits of Exact Science as Applied to History* (London, 1860), p. 17.
[8] *Ibid.*, p. 9.

larged upon ten years later and that have become in recent years the foci of disputes concerning subjectivism and relativism in historical study. Froude argued (1) that the phenomena of history never repeat themselves, thus making experiment impossible in this field; (2) that the so-called "facts" of history are not certain because the historical record is composed of statements made by fallible men; and (3) that, even granting the "facts," each particular historian selects from them to arrive at his synthesis, and any thesis can be supported in this way. The implication that these conditions of historical inquiry seriously undermined the rational character of the enterprise was freely admitted by Froude. Historians should address their works "less to the understanding than to the higher emotions." The vehicle they should employ in conveying their moral message is the drama. The story of "Macbeth," Froude argued quite seriously, provides a model for historical writing, because in this form the historian "can let his story tell itself in the deeds and words of those who act it out."[9]

Despite their characterization of history as a kind of skillfully composed story to point a moral, Smith, Kingsley, and Froude insisted that historians must tell the truth and stick to facts. This was a rule reiterated by most nineteenth-century historians. Revolting against an earlier tendency in their own discipline to let narration slip into fiction, as well as against any form of "sociologizing" that would reduce the particulars of experience to abstractions, they turned with renewed vigor and improved techniques to what Carl Wilhelm von Humboldt had described as their proper function—*die Darstellung des Geschehens*, the description of what happened.[10] Greenwood reminded his students that statements of fact in history must, as in English law, include a distinct specification of time and place; the "times when" and the "places where" were elementary considerations that must bring to the historian a proper respect for the inviolability of the concreteness of historical fact.[11] Ranke resolved to "stick to the facts" and confine himself to telling "what actually happened,"[12] while Karl von Rotteck declared that the "strict and proper signification claims for history merely events determinate as to time, place, and circumstances, conse-

---

[9] James Anthony Froude, "The Science of History," in his *Short Studies on Great Subjects* (New York, 1908), I:14, 17–18, 30–32. See also F. H. Bradley, *The Presuppositions of Critical History* (Oxford, 1874).
[10] J. T. Merz, *A History of European Thought in the Nineteenth Century*, IV:500–501; J. W. Thompson, *A History of Historical Writing*, II:164; Frederick J. Teggart, *Prolegomena to History* (Berkeley, 1916), p. 120.
[11] Greenwood, *op. cit.*, pp. 35–36.
[12] Leopold von Ranke, *Geschichten der romanischen und germanischen Volker von 1494 bis 1514*, 2 Auflage (Leipzig, 1874), p. vii. See also G. P. Gooch, *History and Historians in the Nineteenth Century* (London, 1935), p. 78.

quently only those that happen or have happened, once for all. . . ."[13]

In their eagerness to keep within the solid realm of fact, nineteenth-century historians sometimes forgot, in their definitions of history, the warnings of Froude and Bradley concerning the necessary framework of presupposition that accompanied narration, but the oversight was not apparent in historical writing itself. Annals or chronologies did not replace histories, and historians continued to write from predetermined points of view, select from the data available, and in general show considerable effects of adherence to what others could call a philosophy of history. Sober examiners of what historians were doing did not try to conceal the "synthetic" operation that accompanied and followed a critical and analytical study of documents.[14]

Remarks like Tylor's, however, to the effect that historians seeking to "elicit general principles of human action" were actually pursuing anthropological or sociological objectives, should not obscure the fundamental cleavage that existed between history and social science—at least so far as historians were concerned. Rigid standards of historical scholarship had been set, and the professional historian who disregarded them was quickly detected and banished to the "sociological" category. An interesting case in point is Karl Lamprecht. Until 1890, James Westfall Thompson tells us, Lamprecht followed the conventional pattern of writing history. In 1891 the first volume of his *Deutsche Geschichte* appeared, and for the rest of his life he suffered the wrath of his colleagues in history. Lamprecht had criticized Ranke and his school for emphasizing the individual, for dealing in strictly political events, for failing to seek out the basic causes of progress, and for collecting facts when the establishment of laws should have been their aim. In other words, Lamprecht had raised precisely the same objections to the traditional study of history as had Comte and Spencer. The judgment passed on him was that "he had betrayed history and ceased to be an historian."[15]

Rebels like Lamprecht were rare among historians, however, and it could hardly be argued that they constituted, at least in the nineteenth century, a significant response to the proposed new science of history. Historians remained faithful to the principle that "there is no substitute for documents: no documents, no history."[16] They continued

[13] Karl von Rotteck, *The History of the World*, new ed., rev. (New York, 1883?), I:1.

[14] For a recognition of Ranke's conception of the "universal" in history see Hajo Holborn, "The Science of History," in *The Interpretation of History*, ed. by Joseph R. Strayer (Princeton, 1943), pp. 78–79.

[15] J. W. Thompson, *op. cit.*, II:422–427.

[16] C. V. Langlois and C. Seignobos, *Introduction to the Study of History*, trans. by G. G. Berry (New York, 1912), pp. 17, 213.

to insist on the strict time-and-place character of historical facts, and they never relinquished the view that if history is to be history a narrative "must be kept definite in outline and positive in dates."[17] As Henri Pirenne more recently expressed it, the historian deals in facts which he envisages as "the episodes of a great adventure about which he must tell." His task is to "bring out all that has happened in the course of the ages to make of [social existence] what it has in reality been." Finally, his form of presentation is that followed since the "first existence" of history: "To construct history is to narrate it."[18]

The reaction of historians to the nineteenth-century critique of their activities and to suggestions for a new kind of scientific study of the past has been disappointing, therefore, in view of the methodological issues that might have been raised. As Goldenweiser observed, historians were in the habit of dealing with series of events, and they proceeded to ignore evolutionism.[19] They turned their back on the "historical-comparative" method for the simple reason that it did not involve the use of masses of data about events, and the historians' business was with events. In view of this negative attitude, it can hardly be claimed that historians tested evolutionary hypotheses by bringing historical data to bear on specific questions raised by sociologists and anthropologists. This would have involved meeting the evolutionists on their own theoretical ground and challenging their assertions with evidence, but except in an occasional review or lecture historians refrained from any such venture. The alleged temporal succession yielded by the anthropological or sociological method was not, apparently, a historian's kind of history, and he was not concerned with either proving or disproving it. He regarded it as "not so much true history as the marshalling of types in Aristotelian fashion in their order."[20]

Apart from occasional warnings that a science of human affairs was both impossible and immoral, historians had raised no objections to the

---

[17] James T. Shotwell, *An Introduction to the History of History* (New York, 1936), p. 27.

[18] Henri Pirenne, "What are historians trying to do?" in *Methods in Social Science: A Case Book*, ed. by Stuart A. Rice (Chicago, 1931), pp. 435–436, 441. For a somewhat different treatment of the historian's reaction to nineteenth-century "scientific" history, see John Herman Randall, Jr., and George Haines, IV, "Controlling Assumptions in the Practice of American Historians," in *Theory and Practice in Historical Study*, Bulletin 54 of the Social Science Research Council (New York, 1946), Chap. II.

[19] Alexander A. Goldenweiser, "Four Phases of Anthropological Thought: An Outline," *Papers and Proceedings, Sixteenth Annual Meeting, American Sociological Society*, XVI (1921): 54; "Social Evolution," in *Encyclopaedia of the Social Sciences*, 5:661.

[20] S. Alexander, "The Historicity of Things," in *Philosophy and History, Essays Presented to Ernst Cassirer*, ed. by Raymond Klibansky and H. J. Paton (Oxford, 1936), p. 11.

historical inquiries of anthropologists and sociologists beyond the stubborn remark that these activities did not fall within the definition of academic historiography. Anthropologists and sociologists, on the other hand, were in complete agreement with this judgment. The indictment brought against history by Comte, Spencer, Mill, and Tylor was substantially in accord with the definition of historical study offered by historians themselves. History *was* concerned with narrating, in good literary style, the actions of individuals in time and place, with connecting events causally by reference to the actors' motives, with probing into the "details of this battle or the other seige"; historians *did* construct their narratives around basic themes or philosophies that had a subjective reference and shifted in accordance with a changing intellectual climate. And when historians accused a follower of Comte or Tylor of abstracting from the concrete particularity of experience, of searching for timeless laws of motion, of conceptualizing institutions or processes out of context, of presenting laws that did not apply to the lives of tribes or nations, or of drawing analogies between social and organic or mechanical phenomena, this amounted to no more than a recital of what Comte had set down as the very basis of a scientific approach to the study of man.

The apparent deadlock which historians and sociologists had reached was dramatically revealed when eminent representatives of the disciplines confronted each other at a meeting of the American Economic Association in 1903. Franklin H. Giddings repeated on that occasion some of the criticisms that Comte and Spencer had directed at historians. Noting that the "great bulk of all written history is still frankly chronological in its arrangement," Giddings deplored this "childish" slavery to the simple categories of space and time. A social science must, he argued, go beyond these pigeonholes and classify on a basis of structural and functional similarities. Only then would the "underlying laws and causes" of an orderly process of social evolution be revealed by a "reasoned science of sociology."[21] Albion Small informed the historians present that they discovered things "not worth knowing" and that "somebody else" must bring their crude facts into "meaning relations" if their works were not to remain mere "abortions."[22]

[21] Franklin H. Giddings, "A Theory of Social Causation," *Papers and Proceedings of the Sixteenth Annual Meeting, American Economic Association* (New York, 1904), V:383–386.

[22] Albion W. Small, "Discussion," *ibid.*, pp. 422–423. Small did observe that a "new order of historical work" must fill the "vast void" between our ignorance and the broad sociological theories of causation. *Ibid.*, p. 425. Charles Horton Cooley, another sociologist participating in the discussion, advocated an "organic" view of history—an approach quite like that offered by Comte in his plea for a "philosophic" attitude toward history. *Ibid.*, pp. 426–431.

The response of historians to this indictment could have been anticipated. Willis Mason West pointed out that if historical generalizations ever were made, the man who reached them would be a historian; but West did not believe such generalizations possible. In any event, historians were not going to assume the role of Cinderella in relation to the sister discipline of sociology.

Some of the theorists say to us, "Why you go out, do the digging and grubbing; then bring us what you find, and we will tell you what it means; we will give it 'intelligible order.' " Is it possible these gentlemen wish to dance without paying the fiddler? Or is it simply that they fail to understand how much dancing costs? In any case, there are two good reasons why such a differentiation of function will not come to pass. First, the historians will not take the part assigned; rest assured, if we find anything worth "arranging," we are going to arrange it ourselves, without consulting men who are not historians. And, secondly, we couldn't perform this act of selfeffacement if we would; there are so few periods for which the history is yet definitely established (this is a historical secret, to be spoken in whispers) that only a student trained in historical method and practice can really tell what is good in historical writing and what is not—for the purpose of a final philosophy. And thus, when theorists who are not historians do dip into historical literature to get some basis for their ideal structure, the historians too often are moved to unholy mirth.[23]

The proper relation between history and sociology envisaged by the historians was one of complete separation. "We must let each other alone, with as much charity and good will as may be."[24] George L. Burr observed cooly that "the thing of which Professor Giddings is talking is not history," since the chief aim of historians was simply to learn and tell, in Ranke's phrase, *"wie es eigentlich gewesen ist."* If this was not science, no matter; if it was not knowledge, no matter; it was *history.*[25]

It is evident from all this that two radically different conceptions of the phenomena of human experience existed among Western humanists in the nineteenth century. To historians, the past was a temporal series of concrete happenings whose unique and distinctive characteristics rendered systematic and extensive classification and comparison impossible. To social scientists, the past was process, a succession of forms or structures, in which happenings were conceived as mere manifestations of underlying forces. Historians, in practice if not in theory, admitted the need for imposing some kind of order on the jumble of concrete events. Social scientists, in theory if not in practice, acknowledged the need for relating their statements of process to some sort of historical evidence. But there was no methodological synthesis to bring together the study of events and the study of evolution. The basic problem

[23] Willis Mason West, *ibid.,* pp. 438–439, 441.
[24] *Ibid.,* p. 442.
[25] George L. Burr, *ibid.,* pp. 434–435.

of bringing into conjunction a generalizing operation and the observation of particulars generalized was rendered incredibly complex by a hazy awareness of old and perplexing philosophical problems. In light of the apparent impossibility of arriving at mutually satisfactory solutions to these problems, historians and social scientists could only agree to follow separate paths and "let each other alone." In their indictment of history, sociologists and anthropologists had merely defined the existing practices of historical research and writing. In defending their position, historians simply agreed with the definition.

The consequences of this impasse were manifold. Theories of social change or evolution were never tested (as Maitland had thought they might be) by "men who have been trained in a severe school of history."[26] No light was thrown on Comte's crucial problem of deriving a generalized consecutive series from the historical record. The "historical method" came to mean one thing for historians and quite another thing for social theorists. But important positive conclusions were evident in the dispute. It was, in effect, agreed that historians were doing all that could be done with the *event* content of human experience. A science of man, it followed, must rest upon examination of some other kind of evidence. There might be another dimension of the social past that could be reduced to "law." A lack of regularity in discrete series of unique events would preclude scientific description of such phenomena, but perhaps there was a thread of human experience that lay "in nature" and could be elicited in the form of a "natural history" that would fulfill the requirements of a science. If such were true, then truly there was room for both artist and scientist in the study of man; the subject matter itself dictated the division.

It would be wrong to suppose, however, that these latter conclusions were derived from nineteenth-century arguments between historians and social scientists. The insignificance, in a broader view, of the historian's reply to Comte becomes apparent when we recognize that this conception of the divisibility of human experience into the accidental and the natural was a traditional Western idea. Comte and Spencer had discarded the "individual" as an unscientific datum only on the grounds that there was an independent "general" content to human experience. Tylor's assertion that a science of history must attend to the development of culture rather than of tribes or nations is explicable in terms of the same orientation. The debate with historians only made this point of view explicit.

---

[26] Frederic W. Maitland, "The Body Politic," in *The Collected Papers of Frederic William Maitland*, ed. by H. A. L. Fisher (Cambridge, 1911), III:295.

An appreciation of the grounds on which historians and social scientists agreed to a division of labor must, therefore, be sought in a historical examination of the ideas upon which the separation was based.

CRITIQUES OF THE HISTORICAL-COMPARATIVE METHOD

Objections to the procedures and assumptions involved in nineteenth-century scientific history were by no means limited to the circle of academic historians. In addition to the debates over specific issues noted in the preceding chapter, more basic and constructive criticisms of the historical-comparative approach and the theory of change accompanying it were voiced by several students of institutional and cultural history.

As early as 1852, Sir George Cornewall Lewis delivered a penetrating attack on the Comtean brand of abstract history, argued cogently for a recognition of the plurality of histories, exposed the misleading features of the idea of progress as a conception of social change, and ridiculed origin-hunters who had never learned to respect the significance of a date in determining temporal relationship. Lewis reminded social and cultural evolutionists that if they were really interested in depicting temporal process a large body of dated historical evidence was available for that purpose. To those who seemed bent upon probing only the most remote periods he made the remarkable suggestion that they might well begin with the present and work backward since this would instill a proper respect for the difficulty of reconstructing human history under even the most favorable circumstances.[27]

William Kingdon Clifford, in 1868, struck at the basic presupposition that change is a natural characteristic of culture by calling attention to the persistence and stagnation observable in social institutions, especially in the East.[28] Karl Pearson in his *Grammar of Science* (1892) objected to the indiscriminate arrangement of cultural data drawn from widely separated regions for the purpose of finding chronological sequences. He stressed the need for following "the changes of one tribe or people at a time" and then comparing the results obtained from investigations of several social units.[29] A few years later Franz Boas suggested a similar procedure when he directed his attention specifically to

---

[27] George Cornewall Lewis, *A Treatise on the Methods of Observation and Reasoning in Politics*, 2 vols. (London, 1852), II:390–391. For a more extended treatment of this scholar's strangely neglected contribution see Kenneth E. Bock, "History and a Science of Man: An Appreciation of George Cornewall Lewis," *Journal of the History of Ideas*, 12(1951): 599–608.

[28] William Kingdon Clifford, *Lectures and Essays*, ed. by Leslie Stephen and Frederick Pollock, 2 vols. (London, 1879), I:105–106.

[29] See M. F. Ashley Montagu, "Karl Pearson and the Historical Method in Ethnology," *Isis*, 34(1943): 213.

the "comparative method of anthropology" and recommended a return to the more cautious principles of Tylor and his predecessors. Boas pointed to the abuse of the concept of psychic unity, argued that similar cultural phenomena do not always arise from the same causes, and concluded that the immediate aim of anthropology should be to provide "histories of the cultures of diverse tribes" which could then be compared for the purpose of discovering laws of growth.[30]

Frederic William Maitland approached these questions as a historian. He saw that sociologists and anthropologists were seeking to establish a science of history with biology as their model. With regard to the state, he noted, this orientation must involve some conception of what the normal state is, and we do not know the normal. In constructing his sequences, therefore, the evolutionist was sooner or later confronted with a failure to find what his idea of the normal had led him to expect. The expedients then resorted to were clearly exposed by Maitland: difficulties were explained away on grounds that "the evidence has been lost," or that the unexpected finding is "morbid," "abnormal," a "retrogression," or a "diseased community." All this violated Maitland's standards of historical evidence. It is understandable that a man engaged in the laborious task of searching out documentary evidence on English medieval life should have remarked that he had "a special dread of those theorists who are trying to fill up the dark ages of medieval history with laws collected from the barbarian tribes that have been observed in modern days." But the cruelest thrust was in another direction: "of course," Maitland concluded, "we must not ask the sociologist for anything so unscientific as a precise date."[31]

Among critics of developmentalist assumptions in this period, George Laurence Gomme and Stanley Arthur Cook stand out as figures who discovered the shortcomings of the comparative method in the course of substantive historical research. Gomme, the folklorist, had been quick to seize upon Tylor's doctrine of survivals as a device for converting a mere antiquarian interest into a historical science. But, as he looked into the matter, he came to understand that the connection between contemporary savagery and ancient peoples was not easily established if historical evidence were to be the test. Gomme insisted, therefore, that survivals must be classified before any "premature quest for parellels" was undertaken. This activity led to the observation that survivals in England were not all of the same age, and hence he was introduced to the task of relating various classes of survivals to different periods in

---

[30] Franz Boas, "The Limitations of the Comparative Method of Anthropology," *Science*, 4(1896): 901–908.

[31] F. W. Maitland, "The Body Politic," *op. cit.*, III:385–403.

British history. This work led Gomme to the conclusion that the existence of survivals in modern Britain was attributable to the appearance,
at various times, of arresting forces in the form of invading peoples who
pushed back the earlier residents, who then preserved, in more or less
isolated pockets, elements of their older culture which gradually decayed and reached the status of folklore.[32] Although it cannot be claimed
that Gomme succeeded in this venture, he at least displayed a sensitivity
to the need for dated historical materials relating to a specific geographical area in any project aimed at the discovery of cultural processes.

Cook's attack was from a somewhat different angle. With historical
materials on religions covering a period of over four thousand years, he
found himself in a favorable position for "testing some theories of the
evolution of religion." It appeared at once to Cook that persistence as
well as change was an outstanding characteristic of the institution he
was studying, and furthermore that persistence was not just a quality
of "backward" or "primitive" cultures, but of Western European civilization itself. Inasmuch as he was dealing with very old religious beliefs
that had changed but had at the same time retained many of their ancient forms or had "reasserted" themselves in modified dress and were
still an integral part of the lives of people who held them, the Tylorean
notion of survivals was useless to Cook. Survivals had been defined as
outworn or decayed elements in a culture, vestiges of an earlier phase of
development to be sought only among the backward, the superstitious,
the "folk" in a civilized community. Were religious ideas that had
"survived" for millenia to be regarded merely as the superstitions of
an earlier barbarism? And, Cook asked, *why* have they survived, even
though they be called superstitions?[33]

The type of question raised by Cook and others was bound to cast
serious doubt on a methodological procedure that took continuous and
inevitable change as its only province of study. The comparative method
could not deal with or explain fixity as such; it accepted "obstruction"
to "normal" change as a fortuitous circumstance, incidental in itself,
and important only so far as it provided us with a picture of the past
in the present. Inquiry into a vast segment of human experience was
thus discouraged.

Although this kind of criticism struck at the basis of nineteenth-
century developmentalism and pointed a way to new departures in

---

[32] George Laurence Gomme, "The Science of Folklore," *Folk-lore Journal*, III
(1885): 1–16; *Ethnology in Folklore* (London, 1892), pp. 8–13; *Folklore as an
Historical Science* (London, 1908), pp. xi, 2–4, 10–11, 110–120, 165–176. See also
R. C. Temple, "The Science of Folklore," *Folk-lore Journal* IV (1886): 193–212.

[33] Stanley Arthur Cook, *The Study of Religions* (London, 1914), pp. 49, 129, 131–
n. 1, 174–175, 193, 207 ff., 221–222, 337 ff.

historical method, there is little evidence that it was fully appreciated by the working corps of professional anthropologists and sociologists. What Lewis and Maitland, or Gomme and Cook, had pointed out was that the historical-comparative method was not just an inadequate means for handling historical evidence but actually a device for getting around such data.

The deficiencies of the new "science of history" were not to be sought, therefore, in the formal procedures of that method, but in the larger perspective that had led to its adoption. Repudiation of the contemporary savage as representative of an early stage in culture history did not get to the root of the matter. Rejection of existing cultural differences as equivalents of evolutionary stages did not solve the problem. A science of history would have to take cognizance of the time-and-place particulars of historical experience, and it was the perspective blocking this operation that was responsible for the historical-comparative method and the difficulties in which evolutionists found themselves.

Our general failure to appreciate the basis of our problems in historical study has resulted either in abandonment of an interest in depicting temporal process or in a retention of nineteenth-century evolutionism in disguised forms. It is appropriate, therefore, that we now reëxamine the heritage of assumption that is the source of our dilemma.

PART TWO

The Heritage of Assumption

CHAPTER IV

CLASSICAL THEORIES OF CHANGE

WHY, DESPITE THEIR EXPRESS DESIRE to write "true" history, did social scientists in the nineteenth century fail to use systematically the records of time and place happenings in the experiences of particular peoples? Why did a *science* of society or culture seem to them to preclude a consideration of the concrete events to which historians had traditionally given their attention? On what grounds were the events and series of events in the histories of tribes and nations regarded by both social scientists and historians as unique occurrences about which generalizations could not be made? What pressing considerations compelled sociologists and anthropologists to devise intricate and cumbersome procedures for the indirect reconstruction of history while a rich and unexploited body of direct evidence was available to them?

If the broad theories of social or cultural change advanced in the nineteenth century did not follow upon a methodical examination of historical particulars, how *were* such theories derived? Whence the common notion that slow, continuous, and progressive change was the basic social process? Whence the conviction that nonliterate tribal peoples existing in the present were evidence of early stages in the evolution of civilized European peoples? Whence the detailed criteria of classification or the "principle of arrangement" that made possible the discernment of stages of development in a catalogue of contemporaneous cultural differences?

These questions cannot be answered in terms of the naiveté of nineteenth-century scholars. In the first place, Comte, Spencer, Tylor, or Morgan were not juveniles whose patent errors can be lightly dismissed by a generation of more "rational" social scientists. They were serious and competent students whose vision and industry built a framework within which much of present-day research is carried on. In the second place, the ideas involved were not new to the nineteenth century. Comte and others worked in an intellectual "climate" that they had inherited but had not examined carefully. They already *knew* what science was. They already *knew* what the general course of history had been. The "nature" of society and culture was spelled out for them as an elementary lesson handed down by elders. The relation between their own culture and the recently discovered cultures of distant peoples was fixed for them by the common Western attitude toward the barbarian. Their judgment concerning the artistic and unscientific activities of historians in narrating the singular occurrences in the lives of nations merely confirmed the long-prevalent opinion, shared by historians, that this was the appropriate and only way to handle such data.

Considering the weight and persistence of the tradition they labored under, it is indeed surprising that such men as Comte and Tylor saw clearly, at times, that generalizing statements of social or cultural processes must have reference to the "complication of events" of which record was available in one form or another. But such historical empiricism ran strongly counter to long-standing beliefs about a science of man, and it finally succumbed to those beliefs.

If we are to grasp and deal with these questions as they persist in twentieth-century social science, therefore, we are obliged to examine our intellectual heritage in broader perspective.

Pre-Socratic Conceptions of Nature

Although the formulation of an idea of progress is commonly credited to the seventeenth and eighteenth centuries, and evolution is regarded as primarily a nineteenth-century doctrine, it has been generally observed that preoccupation with the problem of change has been a persistent characteristic of Western thought since the sixth century B.C. "It was a favourite idea with the philosophers of antiquity," wrote Merz, "that everything is in motion, and that the entire process of life and sensation in particular is brought about by the communication and transference of minute movements of a peculiarly mechanical kind."[1] This "deep conviction that everything around us and in us is in a perpetual flux" is usually attributed to Heraclitus of Ephesus, yet it is evident that most Greek philosophers took it as their appointed task to seek out the origin, alteration, and decay of all things and express their discoveries in a broad statement of the process of change. As Windelband pointed out, we find no discussion among early Greeks about the reality or universality of change; they seem to have taken it for granted that an understanding of any thing was to be achieved through an examination of the process of change by which it came to be.[2]

The first answers to the question of change advanced by the pre-Socratics were cast in the form of theogonies. The original stuff was godlike in nature, and its transmutations were conceived and described in terms of personal activities of gods. This religious anthropomorphism represented the world and all things in it as living beings, and the

---

[1] J. T. Merz, *A History of European Thought in the Nineteenth Century* (London, 1907–1914), II:3–4.

[2] W. Windelband, *History of Ancient Philosophy*, trans. by H. E. Cushman, 3d ed. (New York, 1899), p. 35.

process by which many things, or a complexity of phenomena, were derived from one or a few first things was commonly depicted as biological birth and growth in which specific individuals (the gods) provided both material and efficient cause.[3]

With the decline of the older mythology, and the inception of an appeal to reason or science for an explanation of phenomena, the Greek statement of the fundamental problem remained the same. There were, in fact, only minor alterations in the proffered solutions. Cosmogonic poets sought material origins in such entities as Water, Air, Earth, Heaven, Fire, and so on, but they imposed on these natural substances all the attributes with which the gods as originators or creators had previously been endowed. Earth and Heaven were represented as Mother and Father, and a vivid anthropomorphic description of their union for the procreation of all things on earth is a striking feature of the cosmogonies. Again, the elemental substances were frequently conceived merely as opposites that join in an implied sexual union to beget the world and all things in it. The origin and coming-to-be of any thing was still comprehended within a genealogical framework, and the process of change still resembled the growth of a person. So, in Hippocrates, causal factors were no longer referred to the gods, but rather to elemental substances. Yet these substances were regarded as themselves divine, and "Nature" took the place of the gods.[4]

It is not surprising, therefore, to find early Ionic "physiologists" adopting the doctrine of hylozoism—a belief that all matter is endowed with life and spirit. They regarded the world as a living body, and consequently when they turned their attention to the ever-present question of how things have come to be as we find them, they consistently described this process in biological terms.[5]

Nature, thus completely depersonalized, could not so remain indefinitely. Conceived as a power that brings to pass all the events constituting the sum of experience, Nature becomes in fact a Creator and Governor, only deprived of reason and purpose, and identified with the sum of existence. . . . The transfer of the functions and attributes of the ancient gods to Φυσις by the philosophers of the sixth and fifth centuries eventually so charged Nature with personality that the Socratic teleology was a foregone conclusion. From Plato onwards, with few exceptions, philosophers proceed with the synthesis: the gods act according to the laws of Nature, and Nature assumes the divinity of the gods.[6]

[3] *Ibid.*, p. 36. William Arthur Heidel, "Περι Φυσεως, A Study of the Conception of Nature among the pre-Socratics," *Proceedings of the American Academy of Arts and Sciences*, 45(1910) : 83.

[4] *Ibid.*, p. 93 ; Windelband, *op. cit.*, pp. 26–28.

[5] Friedrich Ueberweg, *History of Philosophy*, trans. by George S. Morris (New York, 1903), I :29, 32 ; W. A. Heidel, "Antecedents of Greek Corpuscular Theories," *Harvard Studies in Classical Philology*, 22(1911) : 111–172.

[6] W. A. Heidel, "Περι Φυσεως," pp. 94–95.

It should be noticed, however, that from a methodological standpoint a most significant departure had been made from the older approach to the problem of change. Now it was no longer of importance to speculate on the divine acts that had brought things into being and directed their course in time, no longer necessary to describe the specific happenings that could account for the present situation or condition of affairs. Attention was focused instead on the constitution of things and an effort was made to depict process of change through an analysis of the permanent "nature" of things rather than by a consideration of traditions that narrated the specific acts of certain gods in a presumably chronological order. The early substitution of "science" for myth involved a rejection of historical perspective.[7]

In the field of humanistic inquiry the substitution of natural for mythical explanations had similar consequences. As the search for order and law was extended from the external world to the sphere of human experience, accounts of coming-to-be lost their specific content of mythical deeds and occurrences. Thus Hesiod, despite his appeal to legend, has been credited with construction of a series of developmental stages leading to the human present.[8] "Rational" accounts of cultural advance are attributed to Xenophanes, who denied the participation of the gods in man's acquisition of the arts; to Protagoras, who used the myth of Prometheus merely as a convenient form in which to account for man's gradual elaboration of the mechanical and political arts; to Sophocles, who argued man's ability to progress without direct aid from the gods; and to Euripides, who substituted "intelligence" for "god" in explaining improvement of the fine arts.[9]

These naturalistic accounts of human progress were presented by the Greeks in genealogical form. It was necessary to postulate a first or original state of mankind and follow this with an intermediate series of steps leading up to the present—i.e., the Greek—condition of society. Under the older mythical form of statement this series was composed of gods and divine acts, and the story had an event content. In the new form all attempts at chronology were abandoned, and stages of growth or development took the place of specific happenings.

---

[7] Windelband, *op. cit.*, p. 36.

[8] Andrew Lang, "Edward Burnett Tylor," in *Anthropological Essays Presented to Edward Burnett Tylor in Honour of his 75th Birthday, Oct. 2, 1907* (London, 1907), p. 2. See also J. L. Myres, "Herodotus and Anthropology," in *Anthropology and the Classics,* ed. by R. R. Marett (Oxford, 1908), pp. 127–128; Gilbert Murray, "Anthropology in the Greek Epic Tradition outside Homer," *ibid.*, pp. 66–92; E. E. Sikes, *The Anthropology of the Greeks* (London, 1914), pp. 34–35. That Hesiod presented his Five Races as a series of stages has been seriously questioned, however, by Frederick J. Teggart, "The Argument of Hesiod's Works and Days," *Journal of the History of Ideas,* VIII (1947) : 45–77.

[9] E. E. Sikes, *op. cit.*, pp. 38–40.

EARLY GREEK ANTHROPOLOGY

Need arose for giving some kind of content to these abstract stages, and it was in this undertaking that Greek anthropology is said to have had its beginnings. In attempting to learn how early man lived, Greek thinkers turned first to the Epic poets. Homer did not, however, provide the desired information. Apart from occasional references to peoples lying beyond the civilization on which his interest centered, it was clear that Homer was not describing an original or even a very early system of institutions.[10] Since Homer was the most ancient source available, it appeared useless to look for the history of an actual antiquity to meet the demands of the genealogical presentation. It was common, under these circumstances, for Greek anthropologists to turn to the present and see among contemporary peoples outside Greece an example of the early condition of Greece itself.

Information on non-Greek peoples had been made available by a variety of circumstances. Colonization during the eighth and seventh centuries had carried Greeks from the eastern shores of the Black Sea to Spain and as far north as the mouth of the Rhone. Establishments on the African coast had brought them into close contact with Egypt and Cyrene, and Asiatic Greeks had long been in communication with such eastern tribes as the Phrygians, Lycians, and Carians. As Myres has noted,

The sudden expansion of the geographical horizon of the early Greeks in the seventh and sixth centuries, B.C., brought these earliest and keenest of anthropologists face to face with peoples who lived, for example, in a rainless country, or in trees, or who ate monkeys, or grandfathers, or called themselves by their mothers' names, or did other disconcerting things; and this set them thinking, and comparing, and collecting more and more data, from trader and traveller, for an answer to perennial problems, alike of their anthropology and of ours.[11]

Herodotus has been called the Father of Anthropology because he he amassed an enormous amount of this ethnographic material and thereby laid the basis for later theorizing. It has also been said that in doing this Herodotus remained a mere collector and did not make scientific use of his data.[12] The implication is that he did not generally see in barbarian peoples the cultural progenitors of his own civilization, and that he did not explain the differences he observed in terms of degree of growth achieved. Yet it is important to recognize, if but in passing, that

---

[10] Andrew Lang, "Homer and Anthropology," in *Anthropology and the Classics*, pp. 44–45, 64.

[11] J. L. Myres, *The Influence of Anthropology on the Course of Political Science.* Univ. Calif. Publ. Hist., 4(1916):3.

[12] Sikes, *op. cit.*, pp. 6–7, 10–15.

Herodotus by no means left the question of differences without attempting an answer. He sought repeatedly to explain a given custom by reference to past political events, specific inventions, geographical influences, migration and conquest, and other forms of contact between peoples.[13] No broad theory was derived from all this, but Herodotus does impress us with the multiplicity of factors involved in processes of historical change and stability.[14] Herodotus escaped the strong ethnocentrism of most of his contemporaries.

A much neater organization of the ethnographic data appears in Thucydides. The habit of regarding barbarian peoples as "older" or "earlier" than the Greeks was by now fairly well established,[15] but Thucydides made the first systematic exploitation of the theoretical possibilities in this notion. He began by observing that it was impossible to determine with any certainty the events that preceded the period of which he wrote, but he assumed that "former ages were not great either in their wars or in anything else." Early Greece could therefore be described in negative terms: no regular settlements, no commerce, no accumulation of wealth, no agriculture, no great cities, no walls, no considerable resources, and so on. It seemed to follow, then, that details of that early condition could be filled in by observing the customs of contemporary barbarians or more "backward" Greeks who were most unlike Athenians in these respects. In ancient times piracy was commonly practiced among the Hellenes and was held to be honorable; this was proved by the fact that "certain tribes on the mainland" take such an attitude "to the present day." All Hellenes formerly carried arms; this was deduced from the fact that in some primitive parts of the country (i.e., parts least like Athens) the practice was still followed. Other early customs of dress could be derived from styles prevailing among barbarians and more backward Greeks, and, Thucydides concluded, "many other customs which are now confined to the Barbarians might be shown to have existed formerly in Hellas."[16]

Although these passages on the early "history" of Greece are fragmentary and are obviously not intended as more than an introduction to the theme he had selected, it is correct to say that with Thucydides the comparative method was already complete.[17] Barbarians and non-

[13] Herodotus, *The Persian Wars*, trans. by Rawlinson. See, for example: I:131, 155–157, 171, 173; II:22, 30, 49–51, 79, 91; III:12, 16, 20; IV:46, 67, 76, 106, 180, 189; V:58; VI:58–60.

[14] J. L. Myres, "Herodotus and Anthropology," pp. 134–136; T. K. Penniman, *A Hundred Years of Anthropology*, p. 26.

[15] A. O. Lovejoy and George Boas, *Primitivism and Related Ideas in Antiquity* (Baltimore, Johns Hopkins, 1935), p. 382.

[16] Thucydides, *The Peloponnesian War*, trans. by Jowett, I:1–6.

[17] See Sikes, *op. cit.*, p. 10. Sikes, a defender of the comparative method, is quite explicit in this estimate of Thucydides.

Athenians or backward Greeks were accepted as representatives of an old condition of Athenian culture. The identification was made on the basis of assumptions about ancient Athenian culture, which was, of course, itself the subject of inquiry. Thucydides felt that he had found the ancient history of Greece distributed about him in the present. This thesis had a dual function: it not only served to recover the early history of his own people, but it effectively took care of that great array of different peoples described by Herodotus and others. Now it was clear that such peoples represented antecedent stages in the development of a later and higher civilization epitomized by Athens. The Graecocentric bias of this interpretation accorded well with Thucydides' larger purpose, and it set a pattern of ethnocentrism that later characterized philosophies of history defended by use of the comparative method.

The procedure followed by Thucydides involved the prior acceptance of certain major presuppositions: that change is characteristic of human affairs; that change is slow, gradual, and continuous; that it proceeds through a fixed sequence of stages; and that differences existing at any given time among like units undergoing change result from the varying speeds at which they have moved. Thucydides made no mention of these ideas. It would appear that they were so obvious and so commonplace to him that he did not consider it necessary to establish them as requisites to his mode of inquiry.

If we examine Thucydides' intellectual background to account for his passive acceptance of this important body of assumptions, an explanation is clearly suggested by recalling the principal tenets of the pre-Socratic study of nature. With its background of religious anthropomorphism, this study had endowed the entire physical universe with the qualities of life in a strictly organic sense. All things originated in living matter, and matter contained within itself a principle of change that was pictured as growth. By substituting Culture or Civilization for Fire, Earth, or Water, and endowing the former with biological properties, a theory of cultural change results which accords strikingly with that presupposed by Thucydides' limited application of the comparative method. "Culture" had taken its place among other "natural" objects, and it was to be examined from the same nonhistorical point of view.

ARISTOTLE

The dependence of Greek humanistic inquiry upon the Ionian physiologists becomes more evident upon an examination of Aristotle's masterful summary of earlier speculations on nature and his detailed exposition of what he regarded as the major problems and procedures of scientific study. It is here that we find a firm basis laid for a division between historical and scientific studies.

"Of things that exist," Aristotle wrote, "some exist by nature, some from other causes." Each thing that exists by nature "has within itself a principle of motion and of stationariness."[18] The study of change was emphasized by the observation that the nature of a thing is what it comes to be, so that the form rather than the matter is nature, and the nature is the end or "that for the sake of which" coming-to-be proceeds. "For if a thing undergoes continuous change and there is a stage which is last, this stage is the end or 'that for the sake of which'." Nor is it merely the last stage that is the end, but only the last stage in the sense of the "best." Thus the nature of a thing is to be discerned in the unfolding of its potentiality.[19] This implies that natural processes of change are to be derived from an analysis of potentials in things and not from an examination of what happens to things.

Nature, Aristotle went on to point out, does not work by chance or spontaneity. Just as in the case of intelligent action, nature works for the sake of something, "if nothing interferes." Each different kind of thing comes to be in its own special way, which is the same for each instance of that kind, and "it is not any chance thing that comes from a given seed but an olive from one kind and a man from another." "For those things are natural which, by a continuous movement originated from an internal principle, arrive at some completion: the same completion is not reached from every principle; nor any chance completion, but always the tendency in each is towards the same end, if there is no impediment."[20]

Aristotle had observed that some things are not "natural" in the above sense. Mistakes occur in nature, and the results are recognizable as "monstrosities." The natural includes those things that happen always or for the most part in the same way. But there are also accidental happenings that occur by chance and not for the sake of what actually resulted. He observed, further, that chance events come to pass only as a result of activity on the part of agents capable of moral action when the act performed does not result in that for the sake of which it was performed. Inanimate things and the lower animals do nothing by chance.[21]

What goes on in the world, then, was divided by Aristotle into two

[18] Aristotle, *Physics*, trans. by R. P. Hardie and R. K. Gaye, in *The Basic Works of Aristotle*, ed. by Richard McKeon (New York: Random House, 1941), II:1.
[19] *Ibid.*, II:1–3.
[20] *Ibid.*, II:4, 8.
[21] *Ibid.*, II:4.

sharply defined categories: the natural and the accidental. The distinction assumes importance when it is noted that he was also firmly convinced that there could be no science of the accidental, since "all science is of that which is always or for the most part."[22] It is clear, moreover, that Aristotle was not simply saying that science must seek regularity or commonness among discrete happenings. There are, for him, certain things that are in nature and others that are not. Certain things, it follows, are to be made the subject of scientific inquiry and others are not. His definition of nature provides the means for distinguishing scientific and unscientific subject matter. Any thing, for example, that did not contain within itself a principle of continuous change would be excluded from scientific study. More important, any occurrence in the experience of a "thing" that could not be associated with its true potential would have to be regarded as an accident that need not be comprehended by a scientific description of the thing's natural growth.

Although these observations and Aristotle's doctrine of the four causes[23] might appear quite appropriate to the study of plants or animals (the subject matter that he rather obviously had in mind, as his illustrations indicate) the grave implications for humanistic inquiry can best be appreciated by observing their application in the *Politics*. Here, it will be recalled, Aristotle was studying a group of institutions that he placed in the "natural" category: "the state is a creation of nature, and ... man is by nature a political animal." Inquiry should therefore take the form suggested by the four causes. The material cause of the state must first be determined, for "he who thus considers things in their first growth and origin, whether a state or anything else, will obtain the clearest view of them." Aristotle reasoned that the state is implied first of all in the relationship between male and female. This union, combined with the natural relationship between master and slave, produces a family. A combination of families gives rise to the village. When a group of villages form a single community the state itself comes into existence. This series of stages—family, village, state— or these "parts of the definition," constitute the formal cause. The efficient cause, the primary source or impulse of the change, lies in the natural desire of mankind to leave progeny and to achieve complete self-sufficiency. The final cause, the purpose of the whole movement, or "that for the sake of which" the process was begun and carried through, is the self-sufficient state itself.[24]

---

[22] *Metaphysics*, trans. by W. D. Ross, in *The Basic Works of Aristotle*, XI:8.
[23] *Physics*, II:3; *Metaphysics*, I:3, V:2, VIII:4. See Ueberweg, *History of Philosophy*, I:157–163.
[24] *Politics*, trans. by Benjamin Jowett, in *The Basic Works of Aristotle*, I:2.

Aristotle actually presented a natural history of *the* state, and if we ask, "Which state? Where? When?" the answer must be, again according to his definition of nature, all or nearly all states, everywhere, at all times. If instances are offered where actual happenings present a different history for some state, then the answer must be that the process outlined above is what happens "if nothing interferes" or "if there is no impediment." Or if it be pointed out that most men have never formed the sort of state Aristotle pictured, or did not reach it through the steps he depicted, then we can only be reminded that "monstrosities" can occur in nature and that the man who is stateless by other than "mere accident" is either a "bad man" or "above humanity." It is apparent that Aristotle's science of society is a science of the normal, of what would happen if nothing interfered. The normal, plainly, is not derived from a consideration of all the known experiences of men, but rather from Aristotle's conception of what men should do. Aristotle was engaged here in training the unruly political animal, not in any scientific inquiry.

The actual form of Aristotle's theory of social change was dictated by his use of the biological analogy. If we look about us for objects that are characterized by change, that carry within themselves the source and principle of change, that pass through continuous series of stages that are the same for each individual within a class, that change to realize a potential that exists in the origin or "seed," and that finally "decay" or "come to rest," it is clear that these objects must be organisms—olives or men, to use Aristotle's examples. If we suppose that he regarded the state as an organism, then the form of his inquiry is manifestly appropriate. It would then be essential to consider the state in its "first growth and origin," for that origin would be the seed that contained potentially what the state must, of necessity, come to be. It would also be correct to suppose that every state passes through the same continuous series of stages in its growth. The state, as organism, must also be expected to suffer certain impediments to its growth on occasion—diseases of the body politic that the wise ruler might treat. Finally, by accepting the state as a living body we anticipate its eventual decline and death.

The effect of Aristotle's statement of the problem of social change is to distract attention from the changes that have been recorded in the experiences of men. The "essential" form of natural change must be sought elsewhere because actual experiences include much that happened by chance or accident, which is not a subject of scientific inquiry. Since all natural objects are charged with living, moving forces that direct them purposefully and continuously through a fixed series of stages toward an internally determined end, it must be through a knowledge of these forces that the coming-to-be of anything is to be understood. Substitute "gods" for "forces" here and the progress of Greek speculation on the problem of change seems small indeed.

Besides constituting an argument and example opposed to a historical-empirical approach to the study of social or cultural processes, Aristotle's work also contains the set of assumptions necessary to the employment of the comparative method for reconstructing process. Having accepted the notion that "the phenomenon of 'association' . . . has, like an organism, its normal sequence of stages, from its germinal to its fully developed form,"[25] he could use the "simple," "backward," or barbarian peoples to document early stages in the political development of Greece. Once Greece was accepted as the highest and latest form of political association, and once political association was viewed as fundamentally the same type of organism wherever and whenever it was found, it followed that institutional arrangements different from the Greek must be equivalent to lower or earlier stages in the growth of that civilization. Although Aristotle generally refrained from this sort of documentation and kept his presentation on a highly abstract level, there are enough instances of it in his work to make it clear that he regarded it as a legitimate procedure. Thus he argued that the form of royal rule "still" observable among the barbarians was characteristic of Hellenic peoples prior to their union into states.[26] Again, he pointed out that the "old customs are exceedingly simple and barbarous," and that one of these "old" practices was a contemporary law at Cumae.[27]

Post-Socratic Applications

The theory of change presented by Aristotle, the practice of depicting social or cultural process in the form of a series of growth stages, and the habit of referring to different contemporary peoples for illustration of these stages, persisted throughout the post-Socratic period of Greek and Roman philosophy. Dicaearchus the Peripatetic, a pupil of Aristotle, constructed a series of cultural epochs beginning with an original state of happiness in the age of Cronus, passing through an era of wandering pastoral life, and concluding with a degenerate agricultural period.[28] Varro, in his *De re Rustica* (37 B.C.) echoed Dicaearchus with a richer exposition of the same three stages.[29] Lucretius presented a

---

[25] Lovejoy and Boas, *op. cit.*, p. 174.
[26] *Politics*, I:2.
[27] *Ibid.*, II:8.
[28] Excerpt in Lovejoy and Boas, *op. cit.*, pp. 94–96.
[29] *Ibid.*, pp. 368–369.

detailed account of man's various inventions and cultural advances, although in this instance the presentation was entirely hypothetical, the poet having sought origins only where "reason points out traces."[30] Dionysius Halicarnassensis was among the first to use Celtic data for recovering origins when he commented on the ancient practice of making human sacrifices to Cronus, "just as was done in Carthage so long as the city existed, and as is done to this very day among the Celts, as well as among certain other peoples of the west."[31] Polybius wrote of the natural growth of Rome, and he anticipated its natural decline, just as "every body or state or action has its natural periods first of growth, then of prime, and finally of decay."[32] Seneca used the Scythians and Syrtians to exemplify the early state of nature when everything was provided mankind.[33] And again, Florus, writing in the time of the emperor Trajan, likened the Roman people to an individual man and saw in their history periods of what he called birth and infancy, youth, manhood, or robust maturity, and old age.[34] Finally, Pausanias, in the late second century A.D., turned to his contemporaries in Euboia, Phocis, and Arcadia to recover certain customs of the early Greeks unknown in the historical record.[35]

In some instances non-Greek or non-Roman peoples were used to illustrate an ideal though not necessarily early mode of life. It is only where the ideal condition was identified with an original or early state of man (what Lovejoy calls "chronological primitivism") and a process of degeneration through time was sketched, that elements of the comparative method can be found. Both types of primitivism appeared in the writings of the Cynics and Stoics. But it should be remarked here that a belief in the degeneration of the human race or a theory of cultural retrogression does not bar the use of the comparative method. The method, after all, is only a device for reconstructing history, and if his-

---

[30] *Lucretius on the Nature of Things*, trans. by Cyril Bailey (Oxford, 1910), V:1445–1447. It is difficult to find in Lucretius anything like a series of developmental stages in culture growth. His emphasis on invention and his failure to show how one phase of culture grew out of a directly preceding phase deny him the title of "first evolutionary anthropologist" conferred by Alfred C. Haddon in his *History of Anthropology* (London, 1934), p. 101. Cf. Sikes, *op. cit.*, pp. viii–xi; Lovejoy and Boas, *op. cit.*, p. 234.

[31] Excerpt in Lovejoy and Boas, *op. cit.*, p. 73.

[32] Polybius, *The Histories*, trans. by W. R. Paton (London, 1923), VI:9, 51.

[33] Excerpt from the *Epistulae Morales*, xc, in Lovejoy and Boas, *op. cit.*, pp. 270–271.

[34] Excerpt from the *Epitome Rerum Romanarum*, in Frederick J. Teggart, *The Idea of Progress, a Collection of Readings*, rev. ed., with an introduction by George H. Hildebrand (Berkeley and Los Angeles, University of California Press, 1949), p. 109.

[35] Excerpt from the *Descriptio Graeciae*, VIII:1, 4–6, in Lovejoy and Boas, *op. cit.*, p. 381.

tory is viewed as a process of decline from an earlier, higher state, and examples of that early condition are believed to exist among certain peoples in the present, then the fundamental procedure of recovering origins and intermediate stages is the same as where an idea of progress provides the principle of arrangement. It is quite possible, in fact, to employ the same criteria of arrangement to support a philosophy of progress or of retrogression—for example, an arrangement from the simple to the complex, where different evaluations of simplicity and complexity might be made.[36]

It is equally important to observe that the common Greek conception of cycles, the belief that all things—culture and civilization included—are destined to reach a period of dissolution and decay, neither contradicts the basic theory of change supported by the comparative method nor rules out its particular documentary techniques. The idea of cycles presumes the inevitability of change, and in both its classical and modern forms it pictures change as taking place slowly, gradually, and continually through a fixed series of stages. There is little to distinguish the upward phase of the cycle from the progressive trajectory so far as methodological considerations are concerned. Both present a biological view of change; the cyclical theory simply carries this interpretation to its logical conclusion. Different peoples in the present could be used to document the downward phase of a cycle as well as the upward phase. In the limited schemes of Thucydides and Aristotle, attention was centered on that phase of the cycle between birth and maturity, and their philosophical conviction that this would be followed by degeneration did not distinguish their presentation from later progressive formulations.[37]

CONCLUSION

The use of the comparative method by nineteenth-century scholars to recover and depict the historical past in scientific terms is thus seen not to rest simply on the curious assumption that savages are our contempo-

---

[36] Sikes' remarks on this point illustrate the confusion that so often exists with regard to the assumptions underlying the comparative method. He observes that Greek thought was divided between a belief in progress and belief in a Golden Age. He notes that progress could not be proved merely by pointing to savage society because Greek primitivists could interpret civilization as a sign of degeneracy. Then he says, "but it was more natural to infer that the savage represented an older state of society, from which Greece itself had emerged." *Op. cit.*, pp. 9–10. Leaving aside the troublesome question of just why it was "more natural" to place this interpretation on the evidence, it must be recalled that the chronological primitivist *did* say that the savage (by another, milder name) represented an older state of society. What Sikes apparently means—and this might be implied in his use of the term "emerged"—is that it was more natural to regard the savage as representing an older and *lower* condition of society.

[37] Cf. Sikes, *op. cit.*, pp. 37, 41–44.

rary ancestors. This notion is supportable and can function only within a broad matrix of ideas about the nature of change and the way that science must approach the problem of change. These ideas, in their classical form, are expressed in the following propositions: (1) Change is inevitable; it is characteristic of everything "in nature." (2) Change is slow, gradual, and continuous. (3) Change results from certain fixed potentialities in the thing changing; these potentialities are different for the various classes or kinds of things in nature; but human societies or cultures are universally of the same class or kind and hence all change in the same way. (4) Not all change is "natural," however, for some occurrences are accidental in the sense that they do not result from natural potential. (5) Science studies only the natural. (6) It follows (by implication) that scientific statements about natural change must be derived from an examination of potential rather than the mass of mere historical happenings, since not all of these are "in nature."

Basic to this general orientation in Greek thought was the analogy between social or cultural change and organic growth revealed in the life-cycle of the plant or animal. All of the above propositions can be, and were, derived from the biological analogy. So, when Spencer, in one of his frequent denials of dependence on Comte, remarked that all he and Comte had in common was the conception of society as an organism, he was actually revealing a basic identity in their positions. He was also indicating the traditional source of their theory of social change. For given that conception, their philosophy of change followed, and the comparative method appeared only incidentally as a procedure "above all adapted to any study of living bodies."[38]

---

[38] There is fine irony in Spencer's proud assertion that he knew "absolutely nothing" of the masterpieces of ancient literature in the original and "very little" in translation. (*The Study of Sociology*, p. 415, n. 20.) In another place Spencer did observe that the analogy between individual organisms and the social organism was not unknown in ages past, but he added that "modern science does not countenance those crude ideas of this analogy." ("Transcendental Physiology," in *Essays: Scientific, Political, and Speculative,* I:101.)

CHAPTER V

ORDER AND PROGRESS

SAINT AUGUSTINE

ALTHOUGH IT IS PERHAPS CORRECT to say with Goldenweiser that after Aristotle there were no significant advances in the theory of social change until the seventeenth century,[1] it is difficult to understand the remarkable contribution of that century without considering some intervening events in the history of ideas. Notable among these is the creation by Saint Augustine of the first Western philosophy of history along rational lines.

Augustine's significance for the present discussion lies in (1) the example he furnished subsequent philosophers by seeking law in history through an analysis of "forces" behind historical events; (2) his insistence upon the uniqueness of historical events; and (3) his perpetuation of the classical idea of continuity in change.

Augustine was confronted with the practical necessity of refuting the widely held view that neglect of pagan worship and adoption of Christianity had been responsible for the disasters suffered by Rome. He was also obliged by the requirements of the Christian epic to deny Aristotle's assertion of the eternal nature of the world as well as any cyclical theory of its endless coming-to-be and passing-away.[2] His positive approach to these and other broad questions involved him in a comprehensive statement of the course of human history. The materials, largely Hebraic in source, that he had to use in this undertaking presented him with a detailed chronological account of God's dealings with men. Augustine accepted this account, of course, but he sought more than a bare narrative of events. His aim was to find the true meaning and cause of what had happened, and so to arrive at a prevision of man's destiny consistent with a generalized conception of his past. His objective was the discovery of process in history.

In his search for principles of historical causation, Augustine was obviously predisposed to a monistic interpretation that would present a single cause for a unilinear process. The cause was "God only omnipotent, maker and Creator of the world." God's wisdom and purpose could be discerned in "all being, beauty, form, and order, number, weight, and measure." It seemed incredible to Augustine, therefore, that God's will was not manifest in history, unbelievable "that He would leave the

---

[1] Alexander A. Goldenweiser, "Social Evolution," in *Encyclopaedia of the Social Sciences*, V:657.
[2] Saint Augustine, *The City of God*, trans. by John Healey (Edinburgh, 1909), I:xxxv; XII:x–xx.

kingdom of men, and their bondages and freedoms loose and uncomprised in the laws of His eternal Providence."[3] Augustine's plea for the recognition of law in history as well as in nature parallels in impressive fashion the arguments offered by Comte, Mill, and Spencer fifteen hundred years later.

History, for Augustine, was an orderly process, and he regarded events in that process as manifestations of a force—divine will—that exerted itself from the beginning to realize a definite plan. An event, such as the Flood or the birth of Christ, had meaning only in relation to the over-all scheme of things. Hence the process (or plan, since these were actually the same) could be regarded as prior to the events, and events could be envisaged as results of the process rather than the happenings about which generalizations might be made. It followed that if the plan behind history could be known through direct or indirect access to the intentions or will of the planner, then it would be possible to arrive at a true account of history without attending to what had actually happened, save for purposes of illustrating the *a priori* demonstration. This procedure rested, for Augustine, on the solid foundation of belief that God, the force behind history, had revealed his intentions to man, at least in some measure, through his prophets and his son. Later philosophers of history who looked for "natural" forces behind history could not escape in this way the empirical problem of demonstrating the operation of those forces.

In addition to presenting the view that order, cause, process, or law in history must be sought apart from a consideration of the mere event content of history, and the implied notion that events could be identified in their true form only in the light of some general principle, Augustine is also responsible for introducing to Western Europeans the idea that events in history are unique. His refutation of the Greek idea of cycles and his necessary insistence on the singularity of Christ's appearance compelled him to take this stand. The position seemed to be dictated also by the belief that any repetitiousness in history would suggest a limitation on God's omnipotence or imply that God had acted in vain. Regularity in history, expressible in terms of laws, could not, therefore, imply an orderly recurrence of similar happenings in several times and places. Regularity had to be sought outside events themselves—in the divine will as a historical force or bundle of forces.

Despite his break with Greek ideas on the question of cycles, the form of Augustine's philosophy shows his dependence on classical theories of change. He saw history as a process of change, which he presented in

---

[3] *Ibid.*, V:ix, xi.

genealogical terms. The process had a definite beginning or origin in God's will. Change arose out of the thing that changed, for the principle of good was in man's seed as potential. The change was continuous and the end was approached by finely graded degrees. And it was purposive change, having been intended by God from the beginning.[4] The persistence in Augustine of this mode of conceiving the past in terms of a continuous series of stages or epochs is remarkable when we recall that he started with and was obliged to retain in some way a rich tradition of specific and dramatic events in the history of a people.

CHAIN OF BEING

The Augustinian rationalization of history provided medieval thinkers with a doctrinal answer to the problem of change, but there was another broad area of speculation in which ideas that later became relevant to questions of coming-to-be were expounded. This speculation had to do with the problem of order. Was it possible to discern an orderly arrangement in what appeared to be the unlimited, random multiformity of existence? How could the great *variety* of things in the world be explained? Why did God create so many *different* things? Was there a purpose inherent in diversity? What were the proper and intended relations of all these things?

If all things flow from God, and if God is a purposive, willing agent, it is evident that positive answers to these questions must be given. Although it involved them in serious difficulties, the Church fathers adopted the view that this is an orderly universe, that there exists a fixed and determined relationship among all the classes of things contained in it, and that both the variety and orderly arrangement are good—the best possible. Although this may be a fairly simple proposition in itself, it became enormously complicated in conjunction with the idea of a God who possesses absolutely unlimited powers of creation and arrangement. Without going into the finer points of scholastic logic involved, it led to the assertion that there are no conceivable gaps in the order of creation, that all things can be conceptually arranged in an unbroken unilinear series, and that there is a qualitative continuity in the succession.

Lovejoy has identified the theoretical elements in this view of the universe as (1) the idea that the universe is full ("principle of plenitude"), (2) the notion that there is a unilinear gradation of things comprising the fullness, and (3) a belief that the gradation consists in a continuity of increasing excellence.[5] The "genesis" of the idea of

---

[4] *Ibid.*, X:xiv.
[5] A. O. Lovejoy, *The Great Chain of Being* (Cambridge, Mass., 1942), p. 52.

plenitude is found by Lovejoy in Plato's *Republic* and *Timaeus,* and conceptions of linear gradation and continuity are traced to Aristotle's system of zoological classification.[6] More definite expressions of these views appeared among the Churchmen. Thus Augustine called attention to the necessary multiplicity of kinds of things—"first and second and so on, down to the creatures of the lowest grades"—necessary because "if all things were equal, all things would not be."[7] Aquinas argued that perfection of the universe depended upon the "diversity of natures" in it rather than mere increase in numbers of individuals of a single nature. Albertus Magnus recognized continuity in creation when he observed that "nature does not make [animal] kinds separate without making something intermediate between them," and Aquinas remarked on that "wonderful linkage of beings" in the order of existence.[8]

Faith in the orderliness and continuity of nature was sustained throughout the Middle Ages and Renaissance, so that by the seventeenth century "the conception of order is so taken for granted, so much part of the collective mind of the people, that it is hardly mentioned except in explicitly didactic passages" in the literature of the period.[9] During the eighteenth century the "great chain of Being" was a dominant theme of speculation among philosophers both in England and on the continent.[10] A "world picture" that represented the earth as consisting of a great variety of things had thus been sketched, but no one thing (except God) was supposed to be so different that it would not be possible to find some other almost identical kind of thing. That is, between a stone and an angel there was conceived to exist a finely graduated and perfectly continuous series of minerals, vegetables, and animals. The arrangement of items was made in accordance with some standard of excellence, and those at the top of the series—nearer to God—were definitely regarded as being better than those below them. Moreover, any given member of the series was generally supposed to contain within itself all the attributes belonging to the links in the chain below it. At least, an attempt was made to find an underlying unity amid differences by distinguishing certain general levels of correspondence—for example, in the universe as macrocosm and man as microcosm.[11]

[6] *Ibid.,* pp. 24–66.
[7] *Ibid.,* p. 67.
[8] *Ibid.,* pp. 77–79.
[9] E. M. W. Tillyard, *The Elizabethan World Picture* (New York, 1944), p. 7. A fairly explicit statement of the idea can be found in Sir Matthew Hale, *The Primitive Origination of Mankind* (London, 1677), see esp. pp. 310–311. Lovejoy singles out Leibniz as giving the best seventeenth-century expression of the idea. *The Great Chain of Being,* pp. 144–149.
[10] Lovejoy, *op. cit.,* pp. 59–60, 182 ff.
[11] Tillyard, *op. cit.,* pp. 63, 77, 85, 92–93; Lovejoy, *op. cit.,* pp. 276–277.

Prior to the seventeenth century this set of ideas, the conception of the world as a chain of separate but closely related forms of existence, constituted a static view of the universe. The source of each form or kind was God, and God was supposed to have accomplished the creation all at once. The series was in no sense, therefore, a genealogy.

The seventeenth and eighteenth centuries have been credited with "temporalizing the chain of Being" by regarding the chain as a ladder up which the higher forms had ascended through time, out of a condition represented by present lower forms.[12] Lovejoy explains this modification by pointing to certain logical inconsistencies in the static view, by citing the obvious difficulty of reconciling the theory as it applied to organic forms with the empirical data of biology, and especially by showing how a static view of the universe ran contrary to a belief in progress. This interpretation, though richly documented, leaves many questions unanswered. Why, for example, was the chain temporalized in the seventeenth and eighteenth centuries and not in the fifth, sixth, or thirteenth? Why should a faith in progress suddenly be considered more important or necessary than a belief in order? But, above all, what was there in the idea of a great chain of Being that might have suggested the particular theory of change that supplanted it?

It is a reasonable and attractive argument, of course, to say that the old conception of order had established the principles of gradation and continuity and that the idea of progress finally adopted in the eighteenth century was a theory of gradual and continuous change. There is danger here, however, of regarding the one idea as somehow growing out of the other. The unhistorical character of such a view becomes apparent when it is recalled that the eighteenth-century theory of change was not new, not a recent development, but a persistent feature of Western thought that had been retained even during the Middle Ages in Augustine's philosophy of history. If it is possible to trace the principles of linear gradation and continuity back to Aristotle's scheme of zoological classification, certainly it is as easy to find them in his description of natural change. When change is regarded as growth it takes on the biological characteristics of gradualness and continuity.[13]

Another difficulty in assessing the place of the chain of Being idea in the history of theories of *social* change arises from the fact that different forms of society or culture were not included in the great series.

---

[12] Lovejoy, *op cit.*, pp. 242–287; Tillyard, *op. cit.*, pp. 25–26.

[13] The complexity of this problem becomes all the more impressive when it is recalled that Aristotle's philosophy of change was not derived from and did not apply to his classification of the different kinds of organisms. It applied to the growth of any individual organism and to the history of social institutions.

Ordinarily, man as such occupied a single place in the gradation, and on those few occasions where a distinction was made among men it was on a personal rather than a cultural basis. Thus an attempt was frequently made to find a primate within each class of things in the scale (the dolphin among fishes, the eagle among birds, the lion or elephant among beasts), but in the case of man this amounted to placing the prince or emperor or some highly endowed individual over the common herd. It is true that in seeking to define the highly endowed man Europeans looked to Europe for example, and when interest arose over the missing link between the highest animal and man reference was frequently made to the Hottentot.[14] But man was still regarded as an individual rather than a product of European society, and the Hottentot was not even considered human.

This is not to say, however, that the belief in a great chain of Being stands entirely unrelated to the eighteenth-century study of social or cultural change. Use of the comparative method implied the existence, in the present, of every conceivable form of culture; the "fullness" of the cultural world was assumed. Yet the method itself yielded no satisfactory explanation of diversity. It was applied with the conviction that different cultures existed only because of certain accidents, because certain obstacles had arisen to block the normal progress of various peoples. Some earlier users of the comparative method did refer to a "chain" of cultures and explained diversity and the completeness of the ethnographic record by arguments borrowed from the chain of Being idea—i.e., ultimately from the conception of an omnipotent God. Finally, it is evident that the habit of arranging all the different forms of Being in a series according to some preconceived criterion of excellence provides a model for the first operation in the comparative method—that of constructing a static or coexistent series of cultural forms.

IDEA OF PROGRESS

Modern efforts to found a science of society were dominated by a complete acceptance of the idea of progress. An understanding of the relation of this idea to the use of the comparative and historical methods calls for a brief consideration of its history.[15]

---

[14] Tillyard, *op. cit.*, p. 27; Lovejoy, *op. cit.*, pp. 194, 233–234.

[15] The subject has been dealt with in such works as J. B. Bury, *The Idea of Progress* (London, 1920); Frederick J. Teggart, *The Idea of Progress, a Collection of Readings*, rev. ed., with an introduction by George H. Hildebrand (Berkeley and Los Angeles, 1949); Jules Delvaille, *Essai sur l'histoire de l'idée de progrès jusqu'à la fin de xviiie siècle* (Paris, 1910); H. Rigault, *Histoire de la querelle des anciens et de modernes* (Paris, 1856); Ernest Lee Tuveson, *Millennium and Utopia* (Berkeley and Los Angeles, 1949).

Current analyses of the idea of progress ordinarily stress the substantive content of the notion and neglect the methodological implications of the arguments that led to its acceptance as a theory of social change. Consequently, a later pessimism is taken as evidence that we have rid ourselves of the implications of the idea for procedures in the study of society. Actually the conviction that man and society have been growing better and better and will continue to do so is only one element in the idea of progress, and it is, methodologically, an insignificant element. From the standpoint of the present discussion, the importance of the idea of progress lies in the part it plays in shaping procedures still followed in attempts to arrive at statements of social or cultural process.

In the late seventeenth and early eighteenth centuries European philosophers reached the conclusion that man had advanced intellectually, morally, and materially in the past and that the same progress would continue indefinitely into the future. Taken as a social philosophy, this view may be regarded as an optimistic response to actual changes going on in Europe at this time. Ancient learning had been more fully recaptured, and the scientific revolution had made obvious additions to the store of knowledge. In the secular spirit of the Renaissance, Francis Bacon contemplated the utilitarian purposes to which this new knowledge might be put. Discovery and colonization had vastly expanded the geographical horizon, and with this came not only a sense of new knowledge but also the promise of material gain. And in some quarters, at least, recent productions in art and literature were hailed as evidence that man had reached a higher level of creative genius.

The idea of progress was more, however, than a jubilant expression of hope or self-satisfaction, more than a value judgment concerning the status of European culture. It was given formal statement in an age of science when men deliberately sought unequivocal demonstration of their beliefs. So, the idea emerged not as a faith in the possibility of progress, not as a guarded statement of the probability of future advance, but as an unqualified "law" stating the absolute necessity of continual and never-ending improvement. The way in which this conclusion was reached and the axioms and arguments employed in the demonstration must be examined if the methodological import of the idea of progress is to be defined and appreciated.

In the so-called "quarrel between the ancients and the moderns" during the latter half of the seventeenth century,[16] the moderns contended

---

[16] Evidence has been presented that the quarrel was actually being carried on in Italy a century earlier with music as the arena of discussion. See Warren D. Allen, *Philosophy of Music History* (New York, 1939), pp. 38–40.

that recent achievements in literature, art, or science were superior to the classical heritage. This judgment was not offered merely as opinion. Descartes had written, in 1637, that there are "certain laws established in nature by God," laws that are "accurately observed in all that exists or takes place in the world." If God is the source of natural laws, Descartes continued, then it can be no heresy to say that the world was not "produced at once in a finished and perfect state" but is instead "coming . . . gradually into existence" according to laws of nature.[17] The importance of these views lies in the fact that a deity, whose ways are perhaps mysterious and beyond the grasp of human reason, or who might even act arbitrarily, was now replaced by inexorable laws that operate uniformly in all times and places—laws, moreover, that are discoverable through an appeal to reason rather than to authority.

This principle of "uniformitarianism" was used by the moderns to demonstrate the inevitability of progress. If the laws of nature work with regularity, then men of equal ability must be produced in every age, and mere accumulation of the results of equal efforts will make for advance. Thus Fontenelle argued that there can be no reason for presuming that the brains of the ancients were better ordered than ours. Nature would not be so capricious. "Nature possesses a kind of paste which is always the same, which she ceaselessly moulds and remoulds in a thousand different ways, and of which she forms men, animals, and plants; and certainly she did not form Plato, Demosthenes, or Homer of a finer or better kneaded clay than our philosophers, our orators and our poets of today."[18]

Perrault made the same point: ". . . nature is unchanging and always alike in her productions, and . . . just as every year she yields a certain quantity of excellent wines among a great many inferior and weak wines, she also creates in every age a certain number of superior intellects amid the crowd of common and ordinary minds."[19]

If nature is uniform in her operations and if she works to produce the same effects in every age, then progress, it was argued, is not only a certainty but also a regular, even process. Knowledge advances through accumulation, and the advance is therefore slow, gradual, and continuous. In their effort to characterize this progression the moderns used the old device of comparing the intellectual history of mankind with the biography of an individual. The modern form of this analogy received its first clear statement in Pascal. Scientists of today, he said,

---

[17] René Descartes, *Discourse on Method* (Everyman's Library, New York, 1934), pp. 33–36.

[18] Bernard Le Boivier de Fontenelle, "On the Ancients and Moderns" (1688), excerpt in Teggart, *The Idea of Progress*, p. 176.

[19] Charles Perrault, "A Comparison of the Ancients and Moderns," *ibid.*, p. 191.

are just like those of antiquity so far as their constitution is concerned, but the moderns have profited from both past experience and their own studies. Hence the parallel is suggested: ". . . not only does each individual man progress from day to day in the sciences, but mankind as a whole constantly progresses in them in proportion as the universe grows older, because the same thing happens in the succession of men in general as in the different ages of a single individual man."

The history of the race, therefore, should be regarded as the life of a single man—but a man who "persists forever and learns continually." It followed, for Pascal, that the ancients must represent the "infancy of mankind" and hence do not merit the respect accorded them.[20] Fontenelle, by the vividness of his metaphor, made the biological analogy still more apparent. He spoke of the "infancy," "youth," and "prime" of the "single identical mind which has been developing and improving itself all this time." Again, however, the analogy is not complete, for "the man in question will have no old age."[21]

By these arguments and in this form the moderns contended that it was "natural" for the "body" of human knowledge to "grow"—i.e., to increase slowly, gradually, and continuously in quality and quantity. Their doctrine of the necessity of progress was intimately associated with this particular theory of change. If advance in knowledge had not been regarded as natural and normal, the moderns would have had to inquire into the circumstances and conditions under which advance, stagnation, or retrogression had occurred. This they did not do. The seventeenth-century theorists of progress were, of course, well aware that advance had not, in fact, been continuous. Many of them were rebelling against conditions that they felt prevented progress. The obvious medieval break in European intellectual activity between the classical period and the Renaissance was alone enough to contradict their theory. In order to maintain the notion of continuity they resorted to the Aristotelian doctrine of obstacles. Thus Perrault argued that progress occurs "when all other things are equal"; but when wars, ignorance, and barbarism prevailed the arts and sciences disappeared for a time.[22] Fontenelle maintained that nature worked uniformly to produce men of equal ability in every age, but that the times did not always permit them to show their greatness. Barbarian invasions, universal wars, poor governments, the persistence of superstitions and prejudices, and similar events or conditions prevented the realization,

[20] Blaise Pascal, "Fragment of a Treatise on Vacuum," *ibid.*, pp. 167–168.
[21] Fontenelle, *op. cit.*, p. 184.
[22] Perrault, *op. cit.*, p. 189.

at times, of the progress that would normally take place if there were no such interruptions.[23]

Despite their recognition of a class of historical phenomena that remained unexplained by the thesis of normal progress, men of the seventeenth century chose to accept advance as "that which happens always or for the most part," and to devote their efforts to the construction of an "ideal" history that would demonstate the necessary validity of this interpretation. There was, of course, a lively interest in the "obstacles" to progress, but the point is that obstructing phenomena were not accepted as natural, not as a part of the "real" process of history discoverable by scientific study. To have grappled with the actual historical complexity of change and stability would have been foreign to the purpose of the moderns in the quarrel, and, more important, it would have run counter to their general conception of an orderly universe ruled by simple natural laws and to their Cartesian interpretation of the method and function of science. "The representatives of the Enlightenment of the seventeenth and eighteenth centuries ... were manifestly characterized to a peculiar degree by the presumption of simplicity,"[24] a presumption that left no room for the stubborn time-place events of history.

So, while the philosophers of the quarrel were concerned with a historical question, they did not examine history or write historical works to prove their point. Indeed, they expressly rejected this type of inquiry as unscientific and incapable of deciding the issue. As Teggart observed:

Fontenelle argued that, to arrive at a decision as to the superiority of the "ancients" or the "moderns," it would be necessary to fall back upon the principles of "natural philosophy," if the dispute, conducted by successive appeals, on the one side and the other, to historical evidence, were not to be continued indefinitely. Fontenelle, in short, made a conscious effort to bring humanistic problems within the scope of scientific inquiry, but in this effort he ruled out historical fact in favor of employing the method of science—as envisaged by Descartes.[25]

Historical events, that is, were regarded as beyond the reach of scientific study, while change in time, as a process abstractly viewed, was presumed to be subject to natural laws discoverable through the exercise of an infallible reason carefully employed.

---

[23] Fontenelle, *op. cit.*, p. 183. It is interesting to find Darwin using precisely this argument to explain the interrupted intellectual development of the Greeks when the point was raised in connection with his stubborn adherence to the notion of continuity in change. See his letter to Charles Lyell, March 12, 1860, in *The Life and Letters of Charles Darwin*, ed. by Francis Darwin (New York, 1896), I:88–89.

[24] Lovejoy, *op. cit.*, p. 7.

[25] Frederick J. Teggart, "Turgot's Approach to the Study of Man," *University of California Chronicle*, 28(1926) : 135.

Specifically, Fontenelle avoided an empirical study of history by recommending an analysis of the basic entity that is changing or unfolding in time. This entity was man himself. It is possible, he argued, and "not a bad way of studying history," to conjecture all history, past, present, and future, simply by regarding human nature. This operation leads to the "source of things" and gets at the underlying principles that make possible a "universal view" of all that could have been. Some attention to details, the events of history, he admitted, makes it easier to grasp the general principles and to present them in more agreeable fashion. But the secrets lie hidden in the spirit behind the facts; all events have their source in the springs of the human soul. History, then, should not be an account of revolutions, wars, or the marriages of princes. Attention must be directed rather to the orderly succession of phenomena in the sphere of customs and usages that result from the constitution of the human mind and passions. Orderliness prevails here because all men resemble each other—nature is uniform in human nature.[26]

The quarrel between the ancients and moderns, trivial though the immediate issue might have been, is thus seen to have established an important theory of change and a "scientific" method for studying change, both of which were to exert a profound influence on subsequent efforts to create a science of man. Change was accepted without question as the thing to be studied. Change was described, moreover, in precise terms: it was slow, gradual, continuous, inevitable, and it proceeded infinitely in the direction of the good. The language and concepts used in describing progress were clearly appropriate to a description of organic growth, and the suggested connection was supported by the revival, time and again, of Augustine's analogy between the race and the individual. Finally, the method proposed for reaching and elaborating the theory involved a rejection of historical evidence of changes and relied instead upon a rational analysis of the "nature" of the thing changing.

THE EIGHTEENTH-CENTURY "HISTORY OF MAN"

The comparative and historical method by which nineteenth-century

---

[26] Fontenelle, *Sur l'Histoire*, in his *Oeuvres*, Nouvelle éd. (Amsterdam, 1764), IX: 246–254. Voltaire agreed that a true history must depict the general lines of intellectual progress and not concern itself with the events commonly narrated by historians. "L'objet était l'histoire de l'esprit humain, et non pas le détail des faits presque toujours défigurés . . ." H. Linn Edsall, "The Idea of History and Progress in Fontenelle and Voltaire," in *Studies by Members of the French Department of Yale University*, ed. by Albert Feuillerat (New Haven, 1941), p. 183 [Citing Moland, XXIV: 547, *Remarques pour servir de supplément à l'Essai sur les Moeurs.*]

scholars pursued a "scientific" history of man involved, as we have noted, an arrangement of different cultures or cultural items in a series according to some presupposed principle or principles. The concept of a chain of Being had accustomed men to this procedure of arrangement. The idea of progress provided them with a rough principle of arrangement, for it suggested that cultures could be graded according to the degree to which they resembled contemporary European culture. Europe provided a standard in the construction of a cultural series, just as God had been taken as a point of reference in arranging members of the chain of Being. Underlying both of these notions—the Chain and the Progress—is the idea of continuity. There was supposed to be a qualitative continuity of forms in the present and a qualitative continuity of change through time.

Participants in the quarrel between the ancients and the moderns were concerned with only two terms in a series—the peoples of classical antiquity and seventeenth-century Europeans. They compared certain features of these two cultures, and the moderns sought to depict a transition from one to the other in terms of progressive change. No serious effort was made to discover a condition of arts and sciences anterior to the classical period or to find stages of development between the ancient and modern extremes. The two distant ends of the series were merely connected by a highly abstract theory of change, by a reasoned statement of what must have happened. The gap was left undocumented.

Progress was soon depicted, however, in far more complicated fashion when a scheme of stages, phases, epochs, eras, or sequences was constructed to give a detailed account of the way in which European civilization had come to be. The documentation was accomplished, not simply by reference to periods in European history, but through descriptions of past and contemporary cultural conditions among different peoples in various parts of the world. A striking parallel to this procedure is to be found in the way Laplace supported his nebular hypothesis that the stellar systems had been formed through a gradual condensation of nebular masses. "We see," he argued, "among these nebulae, instances of all degrees of condensation ... and thus we have before us instances of systems in all their stages; as in a forest we see trees in every period of growth."[27] So the student of man was now to find, in the ethnography of the world, cultures in every stage of "growth."

Materials for this operation were provided largely by the great body

---

[27] Quoted in Thomas Fowler, *The Elements of Inductive Logic*, 6th ed. (Oxford, 1894), p. 195.

of voyage and travel literature that appeared in Europe during the sixteenth, seventeenth, and eighteenth centuries. Europeans suddenly came to know the world. Strange new societies of men were discovered in Africa, and especially in America and the Pacific islands. Adventurers, explorers, missionaries, gentlemen travelers, traders, colonial administrators, and naturalists combined to flood Europe with accounts of men in distant lands who differed sharply in their physical appearance and behavior from anything previously known. In some cases the descriptions were surprisingly accurate; in others imagination played a large part; often observation was subordinated to preconceptions of the "savage" or "barbarian" derived from myth or legend.[28]

In any event, the European humanist was confronted with a vast array of physical and cultural differences that called for some kind of explanation. The problem was a disturbing one to men bent upon finding order amid diversity, the simple in the apparently complex. A picture of God's work had been sketched in the chain of Being framework, but now this had to be expanded to include a far greater variety of things than had ever before been imagined. In 1606, Marc Lescarbot stood aghast before the fact that Man, God's fairest work, was not a single thing at all:

Almighty God, in the creation of this world hath so much delighted himself in diversity that, whether it be in heaven or in the earth, either under the same or in the profound depth of waters, the effects of his might and glory do shine in every place. But the wonder that far exceedeth all others is that in one and the selfsame kind of creature, I mean in Man, are found more variety than in other things created.[29]

---

[28] For a bibliography of the voyage literature see T. K. Penniman, *A Hundred Years of Anthropology* (London, 1935), pp. 42–47. African materials have been carefully treated by Katherine B. Oakes, *Social Theory in the Early Literature of Voyage and Exploration in Africa* (Unpublished Ph.D. thesis, University of California, Berkeley, 1944). The debt of anthropology to early travel literature is acknowledged by Alfred C. Haddon, *History of Anthropology* (London, 1934), pp. 102–103. Since the publication of Gilbert Chinard's *L'Exotisme américain dans la littérature française au xvie siècle* (Paris, 1911) and *L'Amérique et le rêve exotique dans la littérature française au xviie siècle* (Paris, 1913), the most detailed examinations of the impact of travelers' accounts on European thought have been in the field of literary history. See, for example, C. B. Tinker, *Nature's Simple Plan* (Princeton, 1922); Samuel C. Chew, *The Crescent and the Rose* (New York, 1927); Robert R. Cawley, *The Voyagers and Elizabethan Drama* (Boston, 1938), and *Unpathed Waters, Studies in the Influence of Voyagers on Elizabethan Literature* (Princeton, 1940). Carolyn T. Foreman's *Indians Abroad, 1493–1938* (Norman, Okla., 1943) gives an interesting account of European reaction to American Indians during their forced or voluntary travels in Europe. John Linton Myres' *The Influence of Anthropology on the Course of Political Science*, Univ. Calif. Publ. Hist. 4(1916):1–81 offers a careful appreciation of the influences of exoticism in shaping European social philosophy.

[29] Marc Lescarbot, *Nova Francia, a Description of Arcadia* [1606], trans. by P. Erondelle [1609] (New York, 1928), p. 145. It is clear that Lescarbot is referring here to the customs and manners of men as well as to their physical appearance.

Robinet, in the eighteenth century, still perplexed as to why God had left man in so many different conditions, offered a similar explanation. Many races remained in savagery "because the productive cause must necessarily fill, with a magnificent profusion, all the classes of animality—must make both domesticable animals and animals incapable of being tamed, savage man and men capable of social life."[30]

Although this explanation of the savage accorded well with the traditional view that God had simply filled the universe with all sorts of things, it still was difficult to reconcile the savage with Genesis and the accepted outline of sacred history. Once it was admitted that savages were actually men and not some species of ape or orangutan, and once the Pope had declared unreservedly, in 1512, that the American natives were descended from Adam and Eve, the ecumenical scope of the Christian philosophy of history required that a place for these strange new peoples be found in the drama of human life. So great were the apparent differences between Old and New World peoples, however, that it was contended by some that if the savages were indeed men, then they were certainly a different kind of men and hence they were not descended from the same pair as civilized man. In 1520, Paracelsus asserted the plurality of races and derived peoples in distant lands from an original pair other than the Adam and Eve mentioned in Genesis. Giordano Bruno, in 1591, declared that "no sound thinking person will refer the Ethiopians to the same protoplast as the Jewish one." The argument was continued in 1616 by Vanini, and in 1655 Isaac Peyrere's famous *Prae-Adamitae* offered the thesis that the first creation took place thousands of years before Adam and that peoples of the New World were not descendants of Adam. In 1721 John Atkyns distinguished separate parentages for the white and black races, and in 1732 an anonymous work, *Co-Adamitae,* attracted wide attention to the view that other men and women, greatly inferior to Adam and Eve, were created immediately after them.[31]

Although these opinions called forth a storm of criticism and counterargument and the monogenist-polygenist debate continued, the belief that different kinds of men peopled the earth did not prove popular. Not only was this idea heretical, but it also ran strongly counter to prevalent notions of the simplicity and uniformity of nature. Man had

---

[30] Quoted by Lovejoy, *The Great Chain of Being,* pp. 273–274.

[31] See T. Bendyshe, "The History of Anthropology," in *Memoirs Read before the Anthropological Society of London, 1863–1864* (London, 1865), pp. 352–360; T. K. Penniman, *op. cit.,* p. 42. The attention given this subject can be judged from the lengthy list of titles refuting Peyrere that is furnished by Fabricius. (Bendyshe, *op. cit.,* pp. 376–377.) See also, bibliography in J. M. Robertson, *A History of Freethought in the Nineteenth Century* (New York, 1930), II:351 ff.

commonly been regarded as a single category in nature, and any evidence or ideas that suggested a revision of this conception were resisted. Confronted with the obviously different in a newly discovered cultural world, Europeans therefore sought immediately to assimilate the unfamiliar to the familiar by concentrating their attention upon similarities between distant or exotic nations and what they knew of Old World peoples through history or contemporary observation.[32] Just as Europeans at first refused to recognize the new geographical horizon and insisted that they had merely discovered the other side of the Old World, so they recoiled from a new cultural horizon and dressed American or Pacific nations in familiar European garb. They convinced themselves that there was really nothing new or different under the sun, that all could be fitted into the old conceptual order, and that strange peoples in faraway places were, after all, basically just like Europeans.

Cultural differences were first accepted, then, merely as a consequence of an omnipotent God who, delighting in diversity, had manifested his power in a profusion of forms. The only comprehensive theory of differences was offered by polygenists. After this, the whole question of differences was subordinated to disputes over the proper explanation of alleged similarities. This basic reaction of a people to the rest of the world has had profound consequences both in the practical arena of European relations with other peoples and in the use to which information about different cultures has been put in seeking a science of man.

Supposed cultural similarities were first explained by Europeans as results of the common racial origin of culture-carrying peoples who had spread over the earth from a single geographical point. Often the specific object here was to refute the polygenetic argument and reconcile sacred and secular history, but complex questions concerning the diffusion of peoples and their cultures and the proper significance of cultural similarities were commonly raised and answers offered. Hence problems of concern to nineteenth- and twentieth-century ethnologists are frequently encountered in the seventeenth-century literature.

A notable effort to settle some of these issues was made by Sir Matthew Hale in 1677. A stout supporter of the monogenist position, Hale began with the observation that the recent discovery of America had "occa-

---

[32] So Tylor, in the nineteenth century, could observe that the ethnographer expected to find similarities, and if an explorer reported something out of the ordinary—not "conformable to the general rules of civilization"—his honesty or accuracy could be questioned. *Primitive Culture*, I:10. Tillyard has presented a vivid picture of the Elizabethan tendency to identify "great correspondences" in their effort to "tame a bursting and pullulating world." "If, for instance," he remarks, "the Red Indian could be referred to men of the traditional Golden Age, their novelty was tamed and they could be fitted into the old pattern and enrich it." *The Elizabethan World Picture*, pp. 92–93.

sioned some difficulty and dispute" touching the common origin of all men in Adam and Eve. The real problem, as he saw it, was to show how the men and animals preserved in the Ark spread to the New World. Unlike many of his successors in the diffusionist tradition, Hale was not content to establish historical connection simply with evidence on similarities. Historical evidence of migration was required. This, unfortunately, was not available, but at least Hale took great pains to demonstrate how the descendants of Noah might have reached America after the flood. He suggested that the New and Old Worlds could have been connected at one time by necks of land, thus providing bridges for early settlers. But he thought it more likely that they came by sea, either purposely or driven by storm. Hale discussed the state of navigation and ships after the flood and concluded that both were sufficiently advanced to permit the voyage.[33]

Having explained the existence of men in the New World, Hale still had to account for their savage condition: i.e., for the fact that they differed so greatly from their European brothers. In brief, he argued that men degenerated with their removal to the New World because of the "ferine and necessitous" kind of life they were required to lead there. Differences of degree of savagery or barbarism among New World tribes were explained by the fact that migrations had occurred at successive intervals since the Flood, and hence some groups had had more time in which to degenerate and forget the "Original" from which they were derived.[34]

This diffusionist position was ably maintained by John Reinhold Forster in 1778. In a work remarkable for its theoretical significance, Forster claimed that cultural similarities, or "parallel customs," are sometimes evidence that the two nations possessing them "owe their origin to one another"; in other cases they indicate that the two nations have a "common origin."[35] Given this orientation, Forster tried to show how various South Seas tribes had migrated from the East Indies. The argument was elaborated and supported by evidence of linguistic, physical, and cultural similarities.[36] This specific case study was offered by Forster in the context of a broader theory of culture history that

[33] Sir Matthew Hale, *The Primitive Origination of Mankind, Considered and Examined According to the Light of Nature* (London, 1677), pp. 177–178, 182–183, 189–195.

[34] *Ibid.*, pp. 318, 195, 197. This explanation of cultural differences in the New World itself is only implicit in Hale's argument. It is a significant innovation in the literature, for differences among American natives were commonly given little attention beyond singling out of the Mexicans and Peruvians as more advanced peoples.

[35] John Reinhold Forster, *Observations Made During a Voyage Around the World* (London, 1778), p. 586.

[36] *Ibid.*, pp. 276–284, 354–360, 401, 535–536, 596–608, *et passim*.

pictured two great systems branching out from their original sources in Chaldea and Egypt—one over India, China, and the East, the other over the West and North. Some tribes, in the tropical or temperate belts, had retained and added to these systems; others, in the interior southern parts of Africa and in most of America, had lost all traces of the heritage. Present differences, then, arose from the fact that some peoples had been forced to migrate toward the poles and had degenerated as a consequence of the harsh conditions of their new life and their removal from the civilizational stream.[37] Here was an implicit denial of any unilinear progress of culture. Forster saw, instead, progress among some tribes, stagnation or degeneration among others, and a belated advance out of the degenerate state by some who had recently reëstablished contact with the main cultural currents.

The cautious search for historical and other evidence carried out by Hale and Forster for the purpose of accounting for cultural similarities and differences was not, however, characteristic of early diffusionism. The position was usually defended by involved argument from Scripture and by "wild speculations" on the meaning of cultural similarities.[38] Thus, in 1721, Fabricius, a strict monogenist, drew on information "copiously noted by learned men in entire and special treatises about the origin of the Americans, the traces of the Old World which have been found in the New, the concurrence of institutions, the comparative proximity of the land of each continent toward the north, the extensive commerce and maritime expeditions of the ancient Carthaginians, and other nations," and concluded that whereas cultural differences did not constitute evidence for multiple origins, cultural similarities did confirm the common origin of man and his spread from a single center.[39]

Although these seventeenth- and eighteenth-century diffusionists offered a formula for linking new and strange cultures to the old and familiar, retained a stress on similarity or uniformity, and presented a genetic or "historical" solution to the problem, still there were implications in their approach that denied a simple picture of coming-to-be. Where an attempt was made to grapple with the actual process of diffusion, as in the case of Hale or Forster, it was obvious that attention must be directed to specific happenings in the migrations and meetings of peoples or cultures. As twentieth-century Boasians were to insist later, the construction of a diffusionist story called for a tedious piecing together of hard-won historical evidence, and even such painstaking

---

[37] *Ibid.*, pp. 295–301, *et passim.*
[38] G. Elliott Smith, *The Diffusion of Culture* (London, 1933), p. 39.
[39] Jo. Alberto Fabricio, *On the Human Inhabitants of Our Globe Who Are of One and the Same Species and Origin* (1721), trans. by Bendyshe from the 2d ed. of 1738, *in* Bendyshe, *op. cit.*, Appendix III, pp. 372–420.

work could at first yield no more than an incomplete picture of the results of contact between specific peoples in a limited area over a short period.

To men steeped in the Cartesian tradition and convinced that scientific laws, like the laws of nature, must be simple, the diffusionist theory seemed more like the discredited type of complicated Ptolemaic explanation of phenomena. They sought, accordingly, for another formula to account for similarities and to use these in reconstructing the broad course of human history. In so doing, they employed ideas that had been familiar to Western thinkers since Thucydides used information about existing "barbarians" to recover the early history of Athens. They decided—to put it in modern terms—that cultural similarities could be attributed to the common nature of man, that they were explicable in terms of independent invention rather than diffusion,[40] and, therefore, that a single history of man or culture could be derived from a conceptual manipulation of cultural differences. Uniformity was thus maintained amidst diversity.

An anonymous essay written in 1695 reflects the current impatience with the diffusionist thesis. Having made the usual observation that striking differences between peoples of the Old and New Worlds render the origin of the latter obscure, the author went on to point out that any argument from similarities to common origin is absurd. The "vulgar opinions of planting all the earth from one little spot" grew out of a "Jewish tradition," and it was deplorable that so many Christians should undertake to prove it. "Every corner," he noted, had been "searched to find out a word, a rite, or a custom, in order to derive from thence many millions of different people. Some will have Norway, others Tartary and China, or some western parts of Africa, to be the sources and seminary of creatures unknown and strange to those climates." The difficulty was that "all nations agree in some words and in some customs; therefore a resemblance in a few of them, is no proof." The only safe conclusion seemed to be that the origins of nations are lost to the human record. "I see no way at present," the author finally decided, "to solve this new face of nature by old arguments fetched from eastern rubbish or rabbinical weeds, unless some new philosopher starts

---

[40] Most histories of ethnological theory refer only to the late-nineteenth- and early-twentieth-century diffusionist reaction to evolutionist theories based on the idea of independent invention and fail to draw attention to the earlier popularity of the diffusion thesis. Notice, on the other hand, that when Boas called, in 1896, for attention to "historical connections" as opposed to "uniform laws governing the human mind," he knew he was advocating a return to an older theoretical position. Boas did not, however, go beyond Tylor for an illustration of this theoretical outlook. Franz Boas, "The Limitations of the Comparative Method of Anthropology," *Science*, 4(1896) : 901–908.

up with a fresh system; in the meantime, let them all be aborigines."[41]

But to let them all be aborigines was to deny the unity of man, and this was not acceptable to eighteenth-century thinkers. Philosophers with an old system came to the rescue. In Lafitau's *Moeurs des Sauvages Americaines* (1724) it was suggested that contemporary customs and manners of Indians presented *"vestiges de l'Antiquité la plus reculés."* Although Lafitau maintained that New and Old World peoples were derived from the same stock, he reasoned that the marked resemblance of early Greek and Hebrew religion to present rites and beliefs of American savages arose from a *"unanimité de sentimens dans toutes les nations."*[42] Apparently, then, an explanation of any given similarity need not be sought in a specific contact or direct common derivation of the peoples involved. People are people—God's creatures—and you could expect to find them behaving in similar ways wherever you found them.

The manifold implications of this point of view for the new science of man were presented by Turgot. In a series of brilliant essays written while he was still a student at the Sorbonne, Turgot sketched a universal history depicting the general progress of man. Genesis, he observed, gives us an account of the origin of man, the invention of the first arts, the Deluge, and the subsequent concentration of mankind in a single family. Following the confusion of tongues, men separated into small groups, went forth into the wilderness, forgot what they had learned, and were "plunged into the same barbarism that we now observe among the Americans." It is from these lowly beginnings that we can trace the progress of the human mind along a uniform path. Having thus distinguished between sacred and secular history, Turgot observed that in the course of the latter various nations have not advanced at an equal pace. As a result of this "inequality varied to infinity," we are confronted in the present with "every shade of barbarism and civilization." Hence it is possible for us to observe, in the present, at a single glance, evidence of every step in human advance, every degree of progress—in short, the "history of all the ages."[43] By these means Turgot traced a unilinear development of man through hunting, pastoral, and agricul-

---

[41] *Two Essays, Sent in a Letter from Oxford to a Nobleman in London*, by L.P., M.A. [London, 1695]. "The second part of the first Essay, concerning the peopling and planting the New World, and other remote countries." Reprinted in Bendyshe, *op. cit.*, Appendix II, pp. 365–371.

[42] Lafitau, *Moeurs des sauvages amériquains, comparées aux moeurs des premiers temps* (Paris, 1724), I:1–26.

[43] Turgot, "Tableau philosophique des progrès successifs de l'esprit humain" [1750], in *Oeuvres de Turgot et documents le concernant, avec biographie et notes*, Gustave Schelle, ed. (Paris, 1913), I:216–217. See also his "Plan d'un ouvrage sur la géographie politique," *ibid.*, I:255–274.

tural stages, with the contemporary American Indian serving as documentation for the hunting phase."

Given this interpretation of recently observed cultural differences, it was clear that a similarity between certain peoples in the present and the historically known remote condition of other peoples was to be expected, for all peoples had common experiences, though not at the same time. When Turgot sighed, "Alas! Our fathers . . . resembled the American savages!"[45] he was merely comforting himself with the thought that the apparent strangeness of savagery really lay in the experience of all men, and, incidentally, that Europeans had done well in raising themselves from such depths to the highest level of civilization. Not only had the "magnificent profusion" of cultural differences been explained, but they had actually been used to construct a historical picture of human experience that placed Europe in the vanguard of the march of the human mind towards perfection. The qualitative ordering of these differences depended, obviously, on a candid acceptance of European culture as the highest known form. The equation of this order with a chronological or historical succession depended simply on the assumption that man everywhere must, by his very nature, move toward a condition represented by contemporary Europe.

The simplicity of this formula, the easy means it offered for dealing with the new diversified world of cultures, the compliment it paid to the Europeans who devised it, and, above all, the tremendous possibilities it presented for the construction of a "scientific" history of man from materials that had hitherto constituted bothersome data that could not be fitted into an earlier conceptual ordering of the human world—all of these circumstances contributed to its quick acceptance by eighteenth-century students. The problem confronting them was like the one that Spencer tells us confronted him a century later when he came to write the *Principles of Sociology:* merely that of fitting a collection of ethnographic data into a scheme lying ready for them.

Among those who set themselves to the task was Cornelius de Pauw. He began with the necessary assumption that Europe occupied an undisputed position at the top of the cultural scale.[46] Next, he made the usual observation that there are great cultural differences between the

---

[44] Turgot, "Plan de deux discours sur l'histoire universelle," *ibid.*, I:278–279, 284.
[45] *Ibid.*, I:304.
[46] Cornelius de Pauw, *Recherches philosophiques sur les Américains, ou memoire intéressants pour servir à l'histoire de l'espèce humaine* (Berlin, 1770) [originally published in Berlin, 1768–69], III:226–227. "... l'Europe est la mère de tous les arts et de toutes les sciences; ... l'Europe est la patrie de tous ces immortel génies, qui ont honoré l'humanité, ou qui l'ont comblée de leur bienfaits. Il faut être un véritable critique pour ne pas avouer cela, ou pour ne pas le savoir."

Old and New Worlds. Why these differences? Because the "germ of perfectibility" that all peoples carry within them has sometimes not grown or has sometimes started its growth at a later period. Since this germ is everywhere the same, however, it is proper to construct, from existing differences, a developmental cultural series. De Pauw presented an economic series rising from the hunting stage through fishing, food-gathering, and pasturing phases to the agricultural era. He subordinated the question of differences to that of similarities, for in order to show that the contemporary savage represents an early stage in European development he was obliged to establish a parallel between the savage and the historical ancestors of European civilization. There followed, therefore, a catalog of alleged similarities of American and ancient Scythian, Gallic, Egyptian, Hindu, and Hebraic customs, religious ideas, superstitions, and so on. Now the question was: Why these similarities? They were not, De Pauw emphasized, to be explained in terms of any connection or relationship among the several peoples. The savage is simply the savage wherever and whenever he is found. Where the needs of men are the same, where the means of satisfying them are the same, and where climatic influences are the same, there customs and ideas will be the same. De Pauw returned to *"ce grand principe"* again and again.[47]

De Pauw had not reached a consistent position from which he could attribute cultural similarities solely to independent invention arising from uniform powers of the human mind. Similarities could still be accounted for by diffusion, though he did not attempt a historical reconstruction along these lines. Adam Ferguson, in 1767, presented a more definitive argument for deriving history from human nature. As Dr. Bryson has shown, the Scottish moral philosophers sought above all to write philosophic or scientific history, and in their search for broad principles of explanation they turned to the basic constitution of man.[48] Nature, Ferguson observed, had given to every animal its mode of existence, its dispositions and manners of life, and she had done the same for the human race. The natural historian must, therefore, examine the properties of this species if he would know what the true history of the species had been.[49]

Ferguson was shrewd enough to see that the nature of man must be sought in the history of mankind, but the methodological dilemma implied here did not actually affect his procedure. He felt that he must

---

[47] *Ibid.*, I:94–101, 113, 139; II:209.
[48] Gladys Bryson, *Man and Society* (Princeton, 1945), pp. 83–84.
[49] Adam Ferguson, *An Essay on the History of Civil Society*, 8th ed. (Philadelphia, 1819 [1767]), p. 7.

start by giving a certain content to human nature before he could begin to deal with the diverse "historical" materials at hand. A criterion was essential to an arrangement of these, and Ferguson provided it at the outset. He assumed that progress was natural to man.

> He would always be improving his subject, and he carries this intention wherever he moves, through the streets of the populous city, or the wilds of the forest. . . . He is perpetually busied in reformations, and is continually wedded to his errors. . . . But he does not propose to make rapid and hasty transitions; his steps are progressive and slow. . . . It appears, perhaps, equally difficult to retard or quicken his pace . . . we mistake human nature, if we wish for a termination of labor, or a scene of repose.[50]

Given this traditional view that it is *in* man to change his culture slowly, continuously, inevitably, and that it is in the direction of improvement (by European standards) that he moves, it is obvious that Ferguson already had a theory of history to which he needed only to add details.

Again we must note that Ferguson consciously discarded the idea of looking for these details in recorded, dated history. He avoided this procedure, not because he was opposed to historiography as such (he wrote a conventional history of Rome), but because he believed he was engaged here, in his history of "civil society," in writing a true history that would reveal "the active spirit of mankind." Early historians of modern Europe had, in Ferguson's judgment, supposed narration to constitute history and had concerned themselves only with events and the succession of princes. He rejected this type of inquiry for his present purposes and sought guidance, instead, from the Greek and Roman historians, those "sublime and intelligent writers" who "understood human nature." Thucydides in particular won his admiration, for it was he who understood that "in the customs of barbarous nations he was to study the more ancient manners of Greece."[51]

The record to which Ferguson turned, therefore, was the literature of discovery, which pictured "almost every situation in which mankind is placed." The original condition of man was sought in the present culture of American savages: "It is in their present condition that we are to behold, as in a mirror, the features of our own progenitors." While Ferguson's principal concern was with this original state, he also marked out a rough distinction between savagery and a "later" barbarism as well as successive stages of social development characterized by hunting, pastoral, and agricultural pursuits. His main series was composed, however, of peoples with the institution of property and those without.[52]

---

[50] *Ibid.*, pp. 11–12.
[51] *Ibid.*, pp. 143–144, 146.
[52] *Ibid.*, pp. 37, 147, 149, 178, 179; Part Second, Section II, *passim.*

Ferguson's case rested, of course, upon the discovery of similarities between present-day savages and the earliest known inhabitants of Europe—since European society was obviously the "civil society" whose history he was sketching. He had little difficulty identifying such similarities, but he was troubled by the thought that likenesses among peoples might result from borrowing or contact. If this were true, the lines of progress would present a tangle that could be unraveled only with information about actual borrowings and contacts among specific peoples. History could not then be derived simply from an analysis of history-as-potential in human nature. Ferguson could not, with candor, deny the fact of borrowing, but he did argue that it did not affect the uniform progress of each nation. He had already observed that art is natural to man. Then "why seek abroad the origin of arts, of which every society, having the principles in itself, only requires a favourable occasion to bring to light?" Similarities exist because men everywhere follow the suggestions of nature. Men do not invent things that they cannot use, nor do they borrow what they are not already prepared to assimilate. "If nations borrow from their neighbours, they probably borrow only what they are nearly in a condition to have invented themselves."[53]

This interpretation permitted the assumptions that each people is capable of unassisted progress, that each will normally pass through the same stages of development, and, consequently, that any given people must represent some stage in the development of the most advanced. The way was open to construction of a hypothetical history of an abstract society through the arrangement of culturally different peoples in an order dictated by the idea of progress.

The writing of such natural, conjectural, or hypothetical histories was a common endeavor of students of man in the second half of the eighteenth century, but the task was not an easy one. The evident shortcomings of the system, the logical inconsistencies, and the hard facts of cultural differences and cross-cultural influences intruded occasionally to demand a patching of the developmental hypothesis. Lord Kames, a contemporary of Ferguson, bent upon writing a history of "Man" could hardly avoid the conviction that this "Man" and his career were not single things at all. Men in various parts of the world were so obviously different that Kames was led to suggest that there were different races, so created by God in order that they might be adapted to the different climates in which they were placed following the dispersion. Beyond this, Kames was disposed to derive the peoples of the New World and

[53] *Ibid.*, pp. 304–306, 156.

Australia from local creations since he found it impossible to share with them the parentage of Adam and Eve.[54] Still, Kames tried to rescue some common denominator for mankind, endowed all men with the same "powers of understanding," and proceeded to the delineation of uniform stages in the development of commerce, writing, religion, economic organization, and in the emancipation of women. His stages were documented by examples drawn from American savages, ancient Egyptians, Peruvians, Mexicans, Greeks, Romans, recent Chinese, and present Europeans—a mingling difficult to justify in the light of the radical differences Kames himself had noted among these nations. Again he recognized the problem and anticipated a later discovery among anthropologists by admitting that his four principal developmental epochs (hunting and gathering, fishing, pastoral, agricultural) had been passed through only by peoples in the temperate zone. And even then he noted that tribes in the temperate zone of North America "oddly" constitute another exception to the rule. This fact, he said, is "singular," but he doggedly added, "there must be a cause, which on better acquaintance with that people, will probably be discovered." The existence of civilized nations in the torrid lands of Mexico and Peru also bothered him, but once more he could only plead his ignorance of America in extenuation of his failure to explain "these wonders."[55]

The new science of human progress, was not, however, placed in serious jeopardy by the recognition of such difficulties. The idea of a unilinear series of stages leading up to the present European society seemed to explain so much, provided such a satisfactory solution to the problem of similarities and differences, and was so agreeable to the high European estimate of European achievement, that recalcitrant facts contradicting the theory were easily disposed of as exceptions or accidents or special effects. Thus, in his *History of America* (1777), William Robertson quickly refuted old arguments that explained the cultural present as a result of diffusion or contact, and firmly announced the sovereignty of the human mind as the controlling factor in history. Since this mind was everywhere the same, then it followed, for Robertson, that history

[54] Henry Home (Lord Kames), *Sketches of the History of Man* (Edinburgh, 1774), I:10, 12, 20, 32–40; II:70–77.

[55] *Ibid.*, I:51–54; II:82–84. We are also indebted to Kames for making explicit the fact that before the comparative method can be employed a principle of arrangement that is itself a theory of history must be adopted. "The science of morals, like other sciences, is in a very imperfect state among savages; and arrives at maturity among enlightened nations by very slow degrees. This progress points out the historical part, as first in order: but as that history would give little satisfaction, without a rule for comparing the morals of different ages, and of different nations, I begin with the principles of morality, such as ought to govern at all times, and in all nations. The present sketch is accordingly divided into two parts. In the first, the principles are unfolded; and the second is altogether historical." *Ibid.*, II:242.

must run the same course among all peoples. Similarity of the Americans to the barbarous nations of the old continent was to be expected, therefore, and likenesses need not be explained in terms of relationship or contact except in those rare cases where strange customs flowed from "arbitrary institution" rather than human nature. In order to distinguish between arbitrary and natural institutions Robertson had to presume, of course, a detailed knowledge of human nature, or of what men do and do not do. By this bold assertion of the oneness of man and hence the oneness of history, Robertson had, in any event, made the American Indian available as a document to "complete the history of the human mind" and to "fill up a considerable chasm in the history of the human species."[56]

Condorcet may be regarded as having given a final splendid expression to the comprehensive eighteenth-century conception of a science of man. In his case again it must be recalled that the great project in the *Esquisse* was undertaken in reaction to traditional forms of historiography. Condorcet criticized political historians for attending to the activities of only a few leading individuals. It was necessary, in his opinion, that we devise a history of mankind as a mass or collectivity. And for this type of history collections of facts were not enough; the facts must be employed with understanding and a philosophical outlook.[57]

A "philosophical" study of man's past involved, for Condorcet, acceptance of the proposition that men's intellectual and moral faculties developed under "necessary and constant" laws that govern all natural phenomena, and the view that human history reveals a slow, gradual progress toward *"la verité ou le bonheur."* He assumed, apparently without the slightest fear that the proposition might be challenged, that Western Europe marked the high point of this progress to date. While he proposed to sketch the development from "the successive observation of human societies in the different epochs through which they have passed," this did not involve, however, a comparison of the histories of a number of societies with a view to generalizing about their experience.

---

[56] William Robertson, *The History of America* (London, 1777), I:266–267, 270–271, 281, 286, 287, 401–402; II:269–270, 298–299, 322. Numerous variations on Robertson's theme appeared around the turn of the century. Of particular interest are C. F. Volney's elaborate derivation of cultural similarities as *"la production naturelle de l'esprit humain"* in his "Observations Générales sur les Indians ou Sauvages de l'Amérique-Nord," in *Tableau du Climat et du Sol des Etats-Unis d'Amérique, Oeuvres,* deuxième édition complète (Paris, 1825 [1803]) and Hugh Murray's highly refined and complicated picture of retrogression and progress and his completely unquestioning acceptance of ethnographic data as historical evidence, in his *Enquiries Historical and Moral, Respecting the Character of Nations, and the Progress of Society* (Edinburgh, 1808).

[57] Condorcet, *Esquisse d'un tableau historique des progrès de l'esprit humain,* in his *Oeuvres complètes* (Paris, 1804), VIII:314.

Condorcet's history dealt with an abstraction—"mankind" or the "human mind"—and so he adopted the expedient of presenting a "hypothetical history of a unique people." Hence he came to regard a variety of different peoples in widely separated places and times as representing stages in the history of a single, "most advanced" nation. These differences could not be arranged as stages, of course, without the original assumption about progress and the acceptance of Europe as a standard toward which all nations were moving. So far, therefore, as they are not purely imaginative, Condorcet's ten great epochs in human history are derived from a manipulation of voyagers' accounts of peoples in distant lands and historical descriptions of nations existing in the past and present. Condorcet shared the peculiar conviction of his predecessors that, taken all together, these various instances of society or culture must form an "uninterrupted chain" from basest savagery to highest civilization.[58]

Condorcet was well aware of the fact that his "law" of social progress did not describe the actual experiences of peoples. He noted, for example, that stagnation was a common cultural phenomenon: many nations remained hunters or fishermen or herdsmen. He even discussed the factors that were responsible for this disinclination to change. Climate might dispose men to idleness. The force of habit—as Bagehot was later to remark—rested heavily on all men. Savages enjoyed an independence peculiar to their condition, and they were reluctant to yield it to civilization. Men were, indeed, "naturally" opposed to the new. They were commonly indolent. Superstition was a widespread deterrent to progress. And, finally, the example that so-called advanced nations had set in their cruel domination of the backward could hardly inspire the latter to progress. He observed, moreover, that progress in the arts depended for its acceleration upon contact and communication among peoples, that what actually occurred within a single nation may be the result of some distant "event."[59]

This frank recognition by Condorcet of a discrepancy between his theory of change and what had actually happened is found, upon closer scrutiny, to have been characteristic of most eighteenth-century "natural" or "hypothetical" historians. Thus, while Turgot firmly believed that progress was a necessary consequence of the nature of the human mind, his observation of exceptions to the smooth upward course of change led him to conceptions diametrically opposed to the assumptions implied by the method of historical study he proposed. He remarked

---

[58] *Ibid.*, VIII:3–4, 11–13.
[59] *Ibid.*, VIII:37–39, 41, 57.

that decadence was frequent, that there had been alternating periods of agitation and calm, that revolutions and other disturbances marked the whole course of history, and that progress actually depended upon the presence of special circumstances.[60] Ferguson, too, observed that the expected results of a natural provision for social advance were not always evident in the experiences of men. Corruption and decline were common phenomena in the history of nations. Stagnation, he noted, had been the lot of others—China and India, for example.[61] Lord Kames' admission of exceptions to the uniform progressive process has already been noted. Robertson's belated recognition of "usages of arbitrary institution" is indicative of some uneasiness in the position of even this most devoted champion of uniform developmentalism.

The way in which these difficulties were handled in the eighteenth-century study of man is instructive in seeking an understanding of the actual objectives of those who pursued a scientific study of history then and in the succeeding century. As discrepancies between theory and empirical-historical fact were noted, fact was simply set aside. After noting the profound effects that invasions, the mixture of nations, conquests, and the dispersion of peoples had had in human history, Condorcet nevertheless insisted that this *"hasard des événements"* must be ignored for the purpose at hand and attention concentrated on changes in a nation apart from such influences.[62] Ferguson argued that divergences from the path of progress were not "natural," did not flow from the "nature of mankind," but rather from men's "voluntary neglects and corruptions." Stagnation must be attributed to the special effects of climate or situation, and not to nature. If a "natural" history were to be constructed, then it followed that the experiences of peoples in "unnatural" or "abnormal" situations must be ignored. As Ferguson put it,

If we mean to pursue the history of a civil society, our attention must be chiefly directed to such examples [of nations enjoying a temperate climate and other conditions of progress], and we must here bid farewell to those regions of the earth, on which our species, by the effects of situation or climate, appear to be restrained in their national pursuits, or inferior in the powers of mind.[63]

It might be argued from this evidence that eighteenth-century nat-

---

[60] Turgot, "Plan de deux discours," pp. 276–277, 285, 302–304. See also his "Recherches sur les causes des progrès et de la décadence des sciences et des arts, ou réflexions sur l'histoire des progrès de l'esprit humain (Fragments)," and "Discours sur les avantages que l'établissement des christianisme a procurés au genre humain," in his *Oeuvres*, I:116–142, 194–214. See also F. J. Teggart, *Theory and Processes of History* (Berkeley, 1941), pp. 183–185.

[61] Ferguson, *op. cit.*, pp. 202 ff., 384, 403; Part Fifth, Sections III–V, *passim*.

[62] Condorcet, *op. cit.*, pp. 40–41.

[63] Ferguson, *op. cit.*, p. 219.

ural historians, as well as their nineteenth-century successors like Comte, Spencer, or Tylor, did not really intend to present generalized statements of the historical experiences of peoples at all. Possibly their efforts can be understood better as attempts to construct from a selection of materials at hand, and with no concern for dated chronology, an ideal series of stages through which qualified nations *should* pass to reach that elevated cultural position achieved by Europeans. That different peoples had not passed through these stages, that the passage had in no historical instance taken place by the gradual and continuous process of change deemed natural, did not constitute an objection to the ideal history. The facts had nothing to do with the case.

Although this might be an accurate description of what was actually achieved, it is also true that the moral philosophers regarded themselves as something more than moralists and felt that they had grounds for saying that what *should* have happened *must* have happened—in fact, *did* happen. They consciously aimed at a "scientific" account of the way in which man, as a result of his very nature, had advanced to civilization. They pointedly referred to their work as "true" history as distinguished from the story-telling and moralizing of traditional historians. Realization of the moral values they held was deemed by them not only desirable but, in the nature of things, necessary. Hence there *must* have been a movement in history such as they depicted, and evidence to the contrary necessarily fell into the category of the unnatural or the accidental, and could not, therefore, be comprehended scientifically. Thus they could regard their picture of human progress as the only really scientific history.

It is a mistake, therefore, to regard these eighteenth-century students as unhistorical in their thinking or to suppose that their aim was merely a delineation of moral objectives for man.[64] Theirs was a serious effort to give an account of the origin and development, through time, of man, society, and social institutions. If their work seems, to historians proper,[65] to violate every rule of the practice of historiography, it must be recalled that the violation was carried out consciously and with the

---

[64] Cf. Hajo Holborn, "The Science of History," in Joseph R. Strayer, ed., *The Interpretation of History* (Princeton, 1943), p. 71: "The old commonplace statement that the eighteenth century was unhistorical has long been discarded. The eighteenth century was one of the greatest centuries of historical thought."

[65] James Westfall Thompson, *A History of Historical Writing* (New York, 1942), II:60, makes the customary historian's judgment of the Cartesian brand of history: "Descartes had a contempt for history, but admirers of his philosophy and his method sought to apply them to history, to political and social institutions, to economics. . . . The eighteenth century was not historically minded. Its speculations concerning the origin of society, of language, of religion, are evidences of this, and in its blind attachment to imagined laws it ignored or denied or defied facts."

conviction that only by the adoption of radically new procedures could the study of human history be raised to a scientific level. As Lévy-Bruhl has pointed out, Cartesians had convinced early modern social scientists that history as it had been practiced could never possess the certainty of mathematics and was at best a "poor little conjectural science," and Malebranche had argued that the mutilated historical record of specific happenings could never yield demonstrable truths.[66] This judgment of the traditional study of history was the stated point of departure in the works of Ferguson and Condorcet, and was retained as a basic orientation for the nineteenth-century founders of sociology and anthropology.

Conclusion

We are now in a position to see that this fundamental methodological point of view was not just a nineteenth-century "aberration of thought," and not merely a lesson drawn from Descartes' *Discourse on Method*. The decision to search for laws or processes of social change by going behind the historical record of changes was based upon assumptions concerning the division of human experiences into natural and accidental categories that are as old as recorded Western social thought itself. The seemingly curious decision of a Ferguson or a Comte to seek generalizations about man's experience by ignoring the particulars to which those generalizations must refer is intimately connected with the Aristotelian dictum that there is an order of human actions that are not in nature, are inexplicable in terms of natural causes, and hence cannot be made the subject of scientific study. The early modern effort to establish a historical science of man rests squarely on the persistent notions that historical events are unique, that science does not deal with the unique, and that a science of history must therefore weave a circuitous route around its proper subject matter.

This perspective on early modern social science, if it is to serve in the detection of problems in the present social studies and an attack upon them, should not be obscured by a myopic attention to the various devices that were resorted to in a search for historical processes when the decision to abandon historical empiricism was made. The biological analogy, the idea of progress, the comparative method, evolutionism, the doctrine of survivals, and theories of diffusion or independent invention assume importance only when the resolve to seek generalizations about temporal process is accompanied by the conviction that the detailed record of temporal process cannot be utilized for such a pur-

---

[66] Lucien Lévy-Bruhl, "The Cartesian Spirit and History," in Raymond Klibansky and H. J. Paton, eds., *Philosophy and History* (Oxford, 1936), pp. 195–196.

pose. More important, when these ideas, devices, or procedures are abandoned, the problems and difficulties in inquiry that they were supposed to overcome remain with us. Either the objective that their users sought—a science of history—must then be abandoned, or a fresh appraisal of the situation is in order and another approach must be tried. In reaching a decision as to which of these courses will be followed, this much, at least, should be understood: the failure of students in the eighteenth and nineteenth centuries to reach verifiable statements about human history was not a failure to elicit such statements from a systematic examination of the time-and-place events in the histories of peoples. Historical empiricism as a way to a science of history was not tried.

PART THREE

Present Difficulties and a Perspective

CHAPTER VI

PERSISTENCE OF OLD IDEAS

THE EFFORTS OF nineteenth-century sociologists and anthropologists to found a historical science of man involved not only the use of technical devices associated with the comparative and historical methods but, more fundamentally, the acceptance of a comprehensive theory of social change and the notion that processes of change must be sought apart from a study of historical events. These substantive and methodological ideas were firmly entrenched and closely associated in the Western intellectual tradition long before the nineteenth century. The extent to which twentieth-century students have liberated themselves from such older orientations will define the character and scope of the task that lies before us.

EVOLUTION

The decision of modern scholars to renounce nineteenth-century evolutionism is based largely on critiques of particular procedures and their associated concepts in the application of the so-called comparative-historical method. There has been a noticeable failure, in the course of this criticism, to penetrate to the matrix of ideas that constitute the theory of social change within which this method could function. In regarding the comparative method as a "curious aberration of thought" on the part of a few eccentric nineteenth-century scholars, we have been content to expose its obvious and superficial errors and have failed to appreciate fully the continued prevalence of the kind of thinking that led men to adopt the method. Althought at least one investigator of this method and its assumptions has been led to wonder "why historians have not taken the trouble to analyze its objectives and its fallacies,"[1] it is generally felt that the issue of evolutionism was properly and adequately laid to rest in the critical writings of such men as Boas, Goldenweiser, and Lowie.

Thus it is commonly observed, as by T. K. Penniman, that attacking the evolutionary school "as it exists today" is like "flogging a dead horse."[2] The procedures of social evolutionists like Spencer and Morgan have, according to Howard Becker, been "thoroughly discredited" and hence "may be dismissed without further ado."[3] More recently, George

---

[1] Gladys Bryson, *Man and Society: The Scottish Inquiry of the Eighteenth Century* (Princeton, 1945), p. 92.
[2] T. K. Penniman, *A Hundred Years of Anthropology* (London, 1935), p. 332.
[3] Howard Becker, "Historical Sociology," in *Contemporary Social Theory*, ed. by Harry Elmer Barnes, Howard Becker, and Frances Becker (New York, 1940), p. 525.

Peter Murdock has assured us that the Boasian school of historical anthropologists "disproved" evolutionism and that "by 1920 evolutionism in the social sciences was completely defunct."[4]

The consequences of this somewhat hasty dismissal of evolutionism have been twofold. First, many twentieth-century sociologists and anthropologists have, in disillusionment, given up entirely an attempt to depict historical processes in society or culture. Frequently this release from an earlier preoccupation has resulted in the discovery and promising exploitation of new research areas—a trend with which there can be no quarrel. In other cases, however, attempts have been made to fill the void created by abandonment of the older objective with piecemeal attention to trivia that proceeds with no theoretical orientation at all. Second, among contemporary scholars who still pursue the delineation of temporal social or cultural process, failure to specify the fundamental weaknesses of nineteenth-century evolutionism has resulted in a retention of those weaknesses. In the absence of probing and constructive criticism, the old theory of social change and its accompanying methodology still exert an unsuspected tyranny. It is with this problem that we are here concerned.

It is becoming increasingly difficult to sustain the judgment that criticisms of evolutionism have either eradicated it as a perspective in modern social science or provided a basis for the construction of new approaches. It is evident, for example, that Lyford P. Edwards conforms to all the rules of eighteenth-century hypothetical or conjectural history in his *Natural History of Revolution,* and makes there the classical assumptions that a study of change must proceed from a theory of human nature and that change is perpetual, slow, and gradual.[5] Dixon and Eberhart's *Economics and Cultural Change* displays the same old concern with "the origin and evolution of the present economic system," the traditional sketching of now familiar economic stages growing out of one another by a process of continuous change, casual acceptance of the proposition that "current primitives" indicate the origins of institutions, and even Adam Ferguson's tattered assumption that the human species changes its culture because it has a "facility" for doing so.[6] Herbert Jennings Rose, in the Frazer Lecture of 1934, stoutly defended the theory of independent invention, attributed cultural similarities to a "like habit of mind" in the "same stage of develop-

---

[4] George Peter Murdock, *Social Structure* (New York, 1949), p. xiii.

[5] Lyford P. Edwards, *The Natural History of Revolution* (Chicago, 1927), see esp. pp. 1, 2, 7, and chaps. 1–2, *passim.*

[6] Russell A. Dixon and E. Kingman Eberhart, *Economics and Cultural Change* (New York and London, 1938), pp. v, 11, 25, *et passim.*

ment of thought and reflection," and so retained a basis for constructing cultural stage sequences by use of the comparative method.[7] Again, it is difficult to see any retreat from the tenets of developmentalism in Géza Róheim's bland assumption that savages do represent our "temporal past" and are our own "still surviving" ancestors.[8] And it must be noted that despite Grahame Clark's use of archaeological evidence in *From Savagery to Civilization,* it is still assumed there that "man" has "on the whole" advanced, that the conception of "evolutionary progress" is still valuable, that "many of the broad speculations of our Victorian predecessors were in essentials true," and, finally, that present savages do represent broadly a condition from which civilization has emerged.[9]

Although these and similar cases may be regarded as sporadic survivals of the older evolutionism, the recent sustained activity of Leslie A. White in reviving and defending the evolutionary thesis cannot be lightly dismissed.[10] Although Professor White has made as bold a statement of the case as could be found in any eighteenth- or nineteenth-century work, and though he has asserted with apparently good evidence that evolutionism has persisted in the substantive writings of its most severe modern critics, the response to his affirmations and charges cannot be said to have demolished the one or refuted the other. Where White has done little more than say that men like Tylor, Morgan, and Spencer were correct in their conclusions and justified in their means of reaching them, his colleagues have only been able to reiterate the arguments that were supposed to have already rid us of this viewpoint.

The strength of White's position apparently stems from his decision to defend above all what we have seen to be the basic methodological proposition of nineteenth-century evolutionists—that history and evolution are entirely different things both in actuality and in study. Whatever stand is taken on the question of similarities, the independent-invention vs. diffusion controversy, the problem of origins, or any of the other minor disputes within the evolutionist context, White can still

---

[7] Herbert Jennings Rose, *Concerning Parallels* (Oxford, 1934), see esp. pp. 9–12.

[8] Géza Róheim, *The Riddle of the Sphinx, or Human Origins,* trans. by R. Money-Kyrle (London, 1934), pp. 255–256.

[9] Grahame Clark, *From Savagery to Civilization* (London, 1946), pp. v, 1, 27.

[10] For this interesting dispute see Leslie A. White, "History, Evolutionism, and Functionalism," *Southwestern Journal of Anthropology,* 1 (1945): 221–248; "Diffusion vs. Evolution: An Anti-Evolutionist Fallacy," *American Anthropologist,* 47(1945): 339–356; "Kroeber's 'Configurations of Culture Growth,'" *ibid.,* 48(1946): 78–93; "Evolutionism in Cultural Anthropology: A Rejoinder," *ibid.,* 49(1947): 400–413; David Bidney, "On the So-Called Anti-Evolutionist Fallacy: A Reply to Leslie A. White," *ibid.,* 48(1946): 293–297; A. L. Kroeber, "History and Evolution," *Southwestern Journal of Anthropology,* 2(1946): 1–15; Robert H. Lowie, "Evolution in Cultural Anthropology: A Reply to Leslie White," *American Anthropologist,* 48(1946): 223–233; Kenneth E. Bock, "Evolution and Historical Process," *ibid.,* 54(1952): 486–496.

insist that if the anthropologist is committed to the study of cultural process, and if he is convinced that historical events are unique, then he is also committed to the construction of evolutionary series by means of an arrangement of observable cultural differences. Given an interest in process and given the view that historical events are not amenable to the sort of generalization implied in process, then White argues in effect that anthropologists are theoretically bankrupt as soon as they leave the evolutionist fold.

The persistence of evolutionism is also evident in recent attempts to support early formulations of the cultural developmental series with archaeological data. V. Gordon Childe has argued vigorously for a study of history that would "yield a science of progress" by utilizing both documentary and archaeological evidence. Since cultural evolutionists have commonly attempted first to establish a sequence in material culture and then to extend this to other culture elements, an archaeologist wedded to a materialistic interpretation of history and in possession of what is apparently chronological evidence of technological advance over a long period finds himself in a position that invites acceptance of the sort of evolutionary scheme associated with the name of Lewis Henry Morgan. Supported in his conviction that technological factors are the most decisive in history "in the long run" by the fact that "Marx pointed out that just these aspects are the most decisive," Childe has proceeded to detect a developmental order in history.[11]

The difficulties that he encounters in this enterprise are reminiscent of the dilemma that has always plagued evolutionists. He is compelled again and again to notice that a chronological classification of undated archaeological evidence, involving as it does the synchronizing of different provinces and some means of handling the problem of "retardation," makes any resulting typology somewhat arbitrary, and applicable at best only to an area covered by a single economic system. He is obliged to hint that some light on the use of antiquities must be gained "by comparison with the implements still being made and used by savages in America and the South Seas." He confesses that "the path of progress looks distinctly erratic" and that a continuous linear sequence appears only when events are viewed "very abstractly." But Childe is most obviously identified with eighteenth- and nineteenth-century evolutionism when he holds that this seemingly uneven course of history presents itself only because it is "distorted" by events lying outside the technological order—the order that he has decided is most decisive in history. He chooses to regard as "vagaries and fluctuations" an appreciable seg-

[11] V. Gordon Childe, *History* (London, 1947), pp. 3, 6, 69.

ment of human experience, and for no apparent reason other than the fact that it does not accord with the theory of progress he has adopted.[12] Despite his reservations and qualifications, it appears that if Childe is left with any statement of human progress it is a statement of what would have happened if what did happen had not happened.

The theoretical position of White and Childe might be regarded in some quarters as ideologically tainted and so not representative of current scholarly opinion. No such judgment is applicable to the social evolution of Robert M. MacIver. Professor MacIver has deplored the tendency in recent years to abandon the concept of evolution and has used it repeatedly in an attempt to introduce students to problems of social structure and change within the discipline of sociology. His explanation of this position might be read in Aristotle or Comte, and MacIver is well aware that his approach is traditional:

The social structure is subject to incessant change, growing, decaying, finding renewal... Its contemporaneous aspect holds and hides the secret of its past. We know its nature, as we know the nature of the living person, only in the comprehension of it through a time-span.... To understand the social structure we must therefore view it in the historical process, seeking continuity, observing also how differences emerge. We must, in other words, discover the direction of change, or all is meaningless. That is why the principle of evolution becomes of supreme significance.[13]

Society, then, is process, and it is MacIver's express aim to find a pattern or general direction in process. Yet he says that his object is not to depict historical change. "We are not," he observes, "undertaking the immense task of tracing the history of mankind or even the history of society. Instead our object is to suggest and exemplify a method of *interpreting* social change." By some means, nevertheless, he discerns process as a mode of change that is "continuous," that takes place in a "definite manner through the operation of forces present from the first within the situation," and that presents itself as a series of transitions through which "one state or stage merges into another." Evolution, as a mode of change, involves everything implied in process, but it also expresses direction and carries connotations of "forward" or "backward" and "higher" or "lower." The latter terms, however, should

---

[12] Childe, *The Bronze Age* (Cambridge, 1930), pp. 56–58; *Progress and Archaeology* (London, 1944), p. 3; *History*, pp. 14–16. There is an apparently considerable alteration of Childe's position on some of the points discussed in his more recent *Social Evolution* (London, 1951). For a detailed critique of Childe's method, see Henry Orenstein, "The Evolutionary Theory of V. Gordon Childe," *Southwestern Journal of Anthropology*, 10(1954): 200–214.

[13] Robert M. MacIver and Charles H. Page, *Society: An Introductory Analysis* (New York, 1949), p. 508.

not impute any standard of valuation, for when this is done we have a concept of progress.[14]

In view of MacIver's declaration that he is seeking only a method of interpreting social change, it is startling to find him remarking, almost parenthetically, that "the process of evolution is objectively given, waiting only to be discovered and understood." But how do we know social evolution when we see it? Borrowing from Durkheim, MacIver provides the answer to this question in his discussion of social structure, where he states that the highly evolved society is one that can include in a common service the variant individualities within it. Or, as he puts it later, social evolution is present in the "history of society" (which he has said he is not presenting) wherever an increasing specialization of organs is discernible.[15]

MacIver thus provides himself with all the principles necessary to an application of the comparative method for the purpose of sketching the pattern of social change "from primitive to civilized society." Although he denies belief in the existence of any unilinear sequence and chooses to speak of "emergence" rather than "origins," when he seeks to describe a condition antecedent to civilized or Western European society he turns at once and without question to the Kwakiutl Indians, the Trobriand Islanders, and the Samoans, using the data on them provided by Boas, Malinowski, and Margaret Mead with the apparent conviction that these materials have been collected for just such a purpose. Looking then to Western European history he finds the later members of his series. This juxtaposition of forms represents for MacIver a process—the evolution of society. "The student of history can," he remarks, "find ample illustration of it in the past." But apparently the historian cannot discover the process, for, MacIver notes, "It would hardly be too much to say that *where we cannot discover an evolutionary element in change, there the past belongs to the historian and not to the scientist.*"[16] Thus the dichotomy between history and evolution and between history and science is maintained.

Another traditional component of evolutionism in MacIver's approach is evident when he seeks to explain the obvious fact that the kind of social evolution he has in mind has *not* taken place. Social evolution, he has said, is a process of differentiation. But he is confronted with the awful example of the totalitarian state, a thriving association in Western Europe in our own time, which has sought with considerable success to stamp out every form of differentiation and individual-

---

[14] *Ibid.*, pp. 512, 521–522.
[15] *Ibid.*, p. 527.
[16] *Ibid.*, pp. 631–633, 522. Italics added.

ity. How is this to be explained? MacIver's answer is that there have been "anti-evolutionary influences" at work in history. The process of differentiation has been subject to pressures directed against it. This countermovement must not be regarded, however, as a part of the evolutionary process. It has occurred only in certain countries where conditions favorable to the process have been absent. These countries "have succeeded only by establishing a coercive control suppressive of the differentiations which *would otherwise arise;* and ... they have occurred as the *sudden* sequel of *catastrophic* and *abnormal events,* not in the more *orderly* course of social change."[17]

It is not the purpose of this inspection of Professor MacIver's sociology to disparage the richness or honesty of a sensitive individual's insight into the role played by the political state in modern Western society. But there is justification for observing that he chooses to present this insight within a framework of ideas about the nature of the historical process that serves to direct attention away from the very problem about which he is concerned. By regarding the totalitarian state as an abnormal phenomenon and by concentrating his attention upon a hypothetical process of social evolution he goes far to defeat the purpose of his study. If his purpose were only to indicate a direction in which he feels we *should* move, then it is quite misleading to present this norm as an objective process of social evolution in time.

Evidence of the persistence of evolutionism despite recent criticism is most striking, perhaps, when it appears in the work of those men who have been its most prominent critics. Robert H. Lowie certainly must be figured among these, and his *Primitive Society* deserves special attention since it is pointed directly at Morgan's *Ancient Society,* which is widely regarded as having been outmoded by the advance of anthropological science.

Professor Lowie, mindful of the difficulties into which classical anthropologists were led by their neglect of history, is convinced that "one kind of relation can never be ignored by the scientific student of culture—the chronological one. ... To put it tersely, whatever else the investigator of civilization may do, he *must* be an historian." He must, Lowie continues, approach his task without assumptions of uniformity in culture history and uninfluenced by any bias for or against regularity in history. Search for all-embracing laws of evolution is a "wild-goose chase," and "a belief in laws regulating the independent reproduction of the same *series* of stages" must be formally abjured. There can be no innate law of social progress, for the extensive occurrence of diffusion

---

[17] *Ibid.,* p. 597. Italics added.

rules out the possibility of historical laws. Hence it is time, Lowie pleads, for the ethnologist to discard old baseless theories and "settle down to that sober historical research involved in the intensive study of specific regions."[18]

A familiar problem arises at this point, however. Lowie is dealing with primitive societies, and they present a difficulty for any one who is determined to be a historian, because events in primitive communities are seldom recorded over a long period. Therefore the ethnologist must have recourse to ethnographic and linguistic evidence and combine this with the data of geographical distribution in order to accomplish a historical reconstruction of culture. It is noteworthy that Lowie now turns at once to a discussion of cultural similarities, submitting them to a classification, very much like Tylor's, in which cultural resemblances found between peoples of different stocks are considered to result either from like causes or from borrowing. Lowie regards the point as an important one, for "sociological laws," he feels, can be inferred only from independently developing likenesses and not from parallels due to borrowing.[19]

Given this familiar orientation toward the problem of similarities, Lowie proceeds to the establishment of temporal sequences. His treatment of the family (a specific point of dispute with Morgan) clarifies his position. After a careful examination of domestic institutions among a wide variety of small non-European communities recently observed, he suggests that the family is present in every "stage" of culture, that at an intermediate level it is often accompanied by a sib organization, while at a higher level the sib is absent. He endeavors to show that the sib appears only when horticultural and pastoral activities have superseded the chase and that it is lacking in "more primitive" tribes. "From this," he argues, "there directly follows the chronological priority of the family." His object is to show that the family is present and the sib absent in the "lowliest" cultures, and his contention is that if this be the case we shall be following the "dictates of reason" in concluding the family to be an earlier and the sib a later development. Evidence that the sib is not encountered in the lowliest cultures (now referred to as the "simplest") is gathered from an examination of tribes in North America, Africa, and Australia.[20]

Lowie then feels that his case will be strengthened if the origin of the sib can be found by seeking factors favorable to the development of the unilateral principle. Finding these in the transmission of property

---

[18] Robert H. Lowie, *Primitive Society* (New York, 1920), pp. 4–6, 337, 432–436.
[19] *Ibid.*, pp. 6–8.
[20] *Ibid.*, pp. 130–132, 147–148.

rights and the mode of residence after marriage, he undertakes to show how they could originate both a patrilineal and a matrilineal community. He examines data on the Hupa and finds there a "germ out of which a father-sib might readily develop." Again, he is interested in showing that the levirate and sororate are older than the sib, in order that the rise of the latter out of action by the former can be demonstrated. The greater antiquity of the levirate and sororate is argued from internal evidence, from their wider distribution, and from the fact that they occur among "not a few of the sibless tribes of ruder culture."[21]

Now, although it must be granted that these and other steps through which Lowie works his way in coming to a decision on the matrilineal-patrilineal issue are certainly guided by a more careful logic than his predecessor's and supported by a more reliable ethnography, the whole procedure depends basically upon the assumptions regarding cultural evolution that Morgan used. Where the techniques for establishing chronological relations do not rest on distributional theories that are questionable at best, they depend upon the proposition that there are discernible among different cultures, grades or levels of civilization, and that the lower are earlier and the higher are later. In order to apply these terms there must be a standard of reference, and it is clear that Western European civilization stands here for the higher and the later. Furthermore, in order to justify the use of data from such a diversity of peoples, it is necessary to assume that, with reference to the particular institutions studied, all these peoples have followed a generally similar course in moving from stage to stage.

The point is not that Professor Lowie is unaware of these objections to his procedure. Indeed, he raises them himself. But he still feels justified in what he does. He agrees that it is impossible to grade cultures from higher to lower in the sphere of social life, but he accomplishes the same thing by arranging material cultures in such a series and then establishing correlations between material culture and institutions like the family or sib and so placing general culture differences in higher or lower levels. He is quite aware that peoples may not advance uniformly in the several departments of culture and that material culture is no certain criterion of social progress, but he simply regards these as legitimate points that can nevertheless be pushed to an absurdity.[22] It remains, however, that whatever objective criteria are employed in ranking cultures as higher and lower, and no matter how positive the correlation between specific culture elements may be, these procedures do not yield *chronological* relationships. They do not provide time *direc-*

---

[21] *Ibid.*, pp. 157, 163–164.
[22] *Ibid.*, pp. 437–439, 149.

tion. This is accomplished only by assuming the "lowliest" and "simplest" to be the "earliest." Sophisticated through this evolutionism might be, it is driven finally to the devices that have traditionally been resorted to by those who would be historians without historical evidence.

Alexander Goldenweiser stands out among anthropologists as perhaps the most perspicacious critic of cultural evolutionism and the comparative method. He recognized clearly that the comparative method could be applied only after evolutionism had been accepted as a postulate and, consequently, that the method could be used only to illustrate and not to test the theory. He realized that evolutionists had to make the assumption that change was gradual and that this notion was derived from the biological analogy. He saw the mistake in identifying diffusion phenomena with the irregular, the accidental, and the disturbing in culture change. He pointed out that parallelism was an axiom necessary to the common use of comparative materials to illustrate evolution. And, what is most unusual in the critical literature of anthropology, he saw that concern with the problem of cultural origins was dictated by the classical belief that origins carried within them the potentialities of what was to follow and so could be examined in order to reveal an otherwise obscure process of development.[23]

It is disturbing to notice that many of these criticisms appear in Goldenweiser's *Early Civilization,* a work in which no chronologically "early" civilization is studied. Early civilization is depicted instead by data recently gathered on the Eskimo, Tlingit and Haida, Iroquois, Baganda, and Central Australian—to whom he refers as "primitive" peoples. A picture of primitive mentality is derived from an examination of Negroes, American Indians, and Australians, and Goldenweiser makes it quite clear that this is "the concrete early man of history and of civilization" that he studies and not some phantom creature.[24] That he sees in contemporary primitives a parallel to an early phase of contemporary modern civilization is evident when he says: "This comparative survey of early industry and art, religion and society, will also enable us to visualize more clearly those peculiarities of civilization which are characteristic of early conditions *as well as* the phases in which the modern and the primitive represent but variants of the common-human."[25]

Aware of the dangers of assuming parallel development and of arranging different cultures to form an evolutionary series, Goldenweiser

[23] Alexander A. Goldenweiser, *Early Civilization* (New York, 1922), pp. 23–27; "Four Phases of Anthropological Thought," *Publications of the American Sociological Society,* 16(1921): 52, 61.
[24] *Early Civilization,* pp. 328–329.
[25] *Ibid.,* p. 131. Italics added.

refrains from placing his five primitive peoples in a series and does not claim that they show parallel trends. Yet he does assume that the "primitive" yielded by an examination of these peoples parallels an early stage in the development of another contemporary segment of the human race which he calls "modern." There is a habit of thought here that disregards simple chronology. When Goldenweiser observes that a certain idea is present in recently observed Polynesian myth and then notes that "in more recent times" the idea was entertained by Greeks and Romans of classical antiquity,[26] he is displaying his casual acceptance of a notion that begs the whole historical question and that lies at the root of the evolutionist procedures he so skillfully attacks.

New departures in theory are always menaced by the unconscious retention of a framework that restricts them and limits the results achievable to an old pattern. An example of this danger can be seen in the vigorous and otherwise promising use of the functionalist orientation in present anthropological and sociological research, where an effort is made to extend the framework to studies of change. Here there are signs of the old fallacy of seeking a short-cut around historical empiricism by attempting to derive process from analysis of structure. Thus, Radcliffe-Brown, despite his plea for observation of actual processes of change, advocates the determination of "what culture really is and how it works" as a necessary preliminary to the study of "how culture changes."[27] Robert Merton's conception of functional analysis seems to involve a similar focusing of attention on selected characteristics of the social structure as "potential" of social change.[28] But even though culture or its parts are to be understood by their functions, functioning is still to be discovered in historical experience. Persistence or equilibrium are as much historical phenomena as change is, and "what culture really is" cannot be discovered outside the historical record. If as functionalists we are to profit from the valuable exposure of some of the earlier malpractices of an uncritical ethnology or sociology, we must beware the basic ideas that led to such malpractices. The danger cannot be avoided if we forget or ignore the repeated effects these ideas have had when men have grappled with problems of change.

The continued adherence of eminent and able men, in their substantive work, to ideas that they have formally rejected, stands as stub-

[26] *Ibid.*, p. 21.
[27] A. R. Radcliffe-Brown, "The Present Position of Anthropological Studies," in *The Advancement of Science: 1931* (London, 1931?), p. 22.
[28] Robert Merton, *Social Theory and Social Structure* (Glencoe, Ill., 1949), p. 42. For a pointed critique of this procedure, see Robert A. Nisbet, "Social Structure and Social Change," *Research Studies of the State College of Washington*, 20(1952): 70–76.

born evidence of the persistent and pervasive character of developmentalist assumptions in recent studies. It is, perhaps, recognition of this situation that has led Murdock to revise his estimate of the death date of these old ideas and observe that historical anthropologists have merely reversed earlier evolutionistic schemes and produced an "inverted image of the very dragon they sought to destroy."[29] It has proved impossible to divest ourselves of an outworn conceptual equipment without understanding that such equipment is forced upon us by a resolve to reconstruct history from a postulate about change rather than from a systematic examination of the records of human experiences.

History

Early modern pursuits of a "true" or "scientific" history of society or culture, which took the form of evolutionism, were accompanied by a hostile rejection of the aims and procedures of historians. This was a conscious rejection, based upon the conviction, inherited from the classical sources of Western thought, that historians deal with events which are unique and hence beyond scientific generalization. Given this estimate of the worth and relevance of the dated evidence of men's experiences, the resolve to sketch general historical processes found expression in an application of the comparative method whereby an arrangement of social or cultural differences in the light of criteria provided by an accepted theory of change was taken to represent a time series. And when the inadequacy of the comparative method led Comte to observe the need for actual historical study he remained so blinded by the notion that events are unorganizable that he did no more than adopt as a philosophy of history the theory of change that he had used in connection with the comparative method. From this point of view, then, the survival or revival of evolutionism and the difficulties into which it leads can properly be regarded as a consequence, fundamentally, of our retention of traditional ideas about the nature of history and historical study.

Thus it is not surprising to find, along with the simultaneous criticism and acceptance of evolutionism, a continued widespread agreement among social scientists, historians, and philosophers that historical happenings are unique, that the accidental and the historical are almost synonymous, and that the specific time-place data of history must, as a consequence, be grasped more in artistic than in scientific fashion. In culture history, we are told, development results chiefly from borrowings during "chance contact," and our civilization has come into being

---

[29] Murdock, *op. cit.*, p. 188.

through a "singular order of events."[30] The "distinction between historical and generalizing sciences"—drawn "long ago by Cournot"—is accepted as a dictum with which we must conform.[31] Kroeber seeks to differentiate between process or dynamics and history, and he chastises Boas for trying to be "scientific" while professing to be a "historical" anthropologist.[32] It is still suggested that whatever is common in cultural phenomena must be discerned as a reflection of human nature rather than in "more or less unique historical experiences."[33] Evans-Pritchard sees the "accidents of history" involved in cultural borrowing as thwarting any attempt to construct developmental laws. Convinced beyond doubt that history and natural science are fundamentally different kinds of studies, he deplores any effort to construct generalizations from an examination of the "succession of accidental events" whereby a society comes to be.[34] Hayek, one of the most energetic defenders of this point of view, condemns the direct search for empirical regularities in social phenomena as "scientism" and is particularly opposed to a "historism" that seeks laws in the "succession of the unique and singular historical phenomena" where, "in the nature of the case" they cannot be found.[35]

Many historians, meanwhile, have steadfastly maintained and elaborated arguments drawn from Bradley, Froude, Kingsley, Dilthey, and Rickert that represent historical study as a subjectivistic, relativistic, presentistic concern with the inviolably singular and individual doings and sufferings of men. They apparently still find it necessary to warn that there is no law or lesson in history, that historical situations do not repeat themselves, and that historical events cannot be bunched or classified.[36] The opinion is re-echoed that we can see in history "only one emergency following upon another as wave follows upon wave, only one great fact with respect to which, since it is unique, there can be no generalization, only one safe rule for the historian; that he should

---

[30] Robert H. Lowie, *Primitive Society*, pp. 440–441.

[31] A. R. Radcliffe-Brown, "The Present Position of Anthropological Studies," p. 4.

[32] A. L. Kroeber, "History and Science in Anthropology," *American Anthropologist*, 37(1935) : 539–569.

[33] David Bidney, "Human Nature and the Cultural Process," *ibid.*, 49(1947) : 391.

[34] E. E. Evans-Pritchard, *Social Anthropology* (London, 1951), pp. 47–49. Evans-Pritchard's argument is not merely that nineteenth-century anthropologists failed in their attempt to arrive at historical generalizations, but also that they could not have succeeded even if they had had historical materials at their disposal. We must recall, however, that early anthropologists agreed with this latter judgment, and because they felt that events of history were accidental they employed the method Evans-Pritchard criticizes.

[35] F. A. v. Hayek, "Scientism and the Study of Society," *Economica*, 10(1943) : 42–43, 58.

[36] Jacques Barzun, "History, Popular and Unpopular," in *The Interpretation of History*, ed. by Joseph R. Strayer (Princeton, 1943), pp. 49–51.

recognize in the development of human destinies the play of the contingent and the unforeseen."[37]

We are still reminded that "facts" are of two kinds—historical and scientific; that historical facts are not repetitive; that man's freedom of will renders a science of history impossible; that the study of history must therefore be more an art than a science; that historians proper must always be concerned with the individual phenomenon; and that historical method "is to tell the story of that individual."[38]

Some historians, ably supported by philosophers, have now gone much farther than this in their enthusiastic agreement with the accusations once hurled at their discipline by Comte and Spencer. In the critical writings of such men as Croce, Collingwood, Beard, and Becker[39] not only are the final products of historical research identified as little more than a disciplined subjective reaction to a body of data selected in accordance with standards individual to the given historian, but the data themsleves—all historical records—are said to have no substance other than that imparted to them by the thought of the individual historian. The liberty of the historian in writing about the past, the utter privacy of his thoughts, are so zealously guarded by this philosophy that any remaining vestige of a public or scientific quality in the historical enterprise is indeed jeopardized.[40]

These conceptions of the historical dimension of human experience and the way in which it must be approached continue to exert a pro-

[37] Henry John Randall, *The Creative Centuries* (London, 1945), p. xv [quoting Fisher].

[38] Edward Maslin Hulme, *History and Its Neighbors* (Oxford, 1942), pp. 10–14, 156.

[39] See Benedetto Croce, *Theory and History of Historiography*, trans. by Douglas Ainslie (London, 1921); *History as the Story of Liberty* (New York, 1941); R. G. Collingwood, *The Idea of History* (Oxford, 1946); Charles A. Beard, "Written History as an Act of Faith," *American Historical Review*, 39(1934): 219–231; "That Noble Dream," *ibid.*, 41(1935): 74–87; "Review of the Problem of Historical Knowledge, an Answer to Relativism," *ibid.*, 44(1939): 571–572; Charles A. Beard and Alfred Vagts, "Currents of Thought in Historiography," *ibid.*, 42(1937): 460–483; Carl L. Becker, *Everyman His Own Historian* (New York, 1935). A more moderate statement by Beard appeared in his "Grounds for a Reconsideration of Historiography," in *Theory and Practice in Historical Study*, Bulletin 54 of the Social Science Research Council (New York, 1946). Beard notes here (p. 11) that historians concern themselves too much with the uniqueness of events and personalities, but he adds that they are bound to exercise this concern owing to "the very nature of history as actuality."

[40] For reactions against this point of view, see Maurice Mandelbaum, *The Problem of Historical Knowledge* (New York, 1938); Arthur O. Lovejoy, "Present Standpoints and Past History," *The Journal of Philosophy*, 36(1939): 477–489; J. R. M. Butler, *The Present Need for History* (Cambridge, 1949); Chester M. Destler, "Some Observations on Contemporary Historical Theory," *American Historical Review*, 55(1950): 503–539. In light of the intricacies of arguments as to whether history is science or not, one can sympathize with Gaetano Salvemini's reference to some of these works of disputation as "fog factories"; see his *Historian and Scientist* (Cambridge, 1939), p. 33.

found influence on the aims and procedures of social scientists. Some have sought to win for their own disciplines the same sort of "freedom" in historical reconstruction that historians have claimed. Tylor argued that the historian proper actually depends on a philosophy of history in his supposedly strict chronological presentations, and that an anthropologist might therefore be permitted some license. The point is revived by Kroeber when he maintains that the distinctive features of the historical approach are "an attitude of mind," "an endeavor at descriptive integration," "an interpretation by means of description in terms of context," rather than a preoccupation with documentation, time sequences, or space factors. Thus the same moot philosophical problems confront historians and anthropologists, and in addition the latter face the difficulty of trying "to do time history for the poor dateless primitives." Resistance to this state of affairs in anthropology, or dissatisfaction with it, is identified, by Kroeber, with the futile effort to mix history and science.[41]

This attitude towards historical study, so ably represented and acted upon by Kroeber, does involve a frank acceptance of historical materials and an attempt to cope with them. There is more common adherence, however, to the nineteenth-century view that if history commits us to mere subjective interpretations then social *science* must somehow trace a course around history and avoid "anything so unscientific as a precise date." We have, as Lévy-Bruhl observes, plentiful variations on the Cartesian theme that since history cannot be exact it is not science; that it is futile to spend our time perusing old records because whatever is extracted from them can have no scientific value, since it cannot be demonstrated in any proper sense.[42]

So, we are confronted with the following type of argument:

We cannot escape history, and we do not want to escape it, because all events that have occurred at all are *ipso facto* history, including yesterday's chemistry experiment. You will notice, however, that the other sciences, in reconstructing the history of the physical universe, have illumined their subject more through the knowledge of contemporary science than through the perusal of ancient documents. The history of the physical universe consists largely of what physicists today say *must* have happened in view of what we know *can* happen and *is* happening. Human history on the other hand, we seem to feel, is more like some kinds of cheese and wine—the older it is the better it is.[43]

[41] A. L. Kroeber, "History and Evolution," p. 4; "Kinship and History," *American Anthropologist* 38(1936): 11; "History and Science in Anthropology," pp. 546–548, 558. For agreement with this view, see David Bidney, "On the So-Called Anti-Evolutionist Fallacy," p. 296 *et passim*, and Evans-Pritchard, *op. cit.*, p. 61.

[42] Lucien Lévy-Bruhl, "The Cartesian Spirit in History," in *Philosophy and History*, ed. by Raymond Klibansky and H. J. Paton (Oxford, 1936), pp. 191, 195.

[43] George A. Lundberg, *"Can Science Save Us?"* (New York, 1947), p. 73.

While the familiarity of the idea presented here would suggest that its author seems to feel that the older a methodological concept for social science is the better it is, there is, nevertheless, a widely entertained notion in contemporary thought than an intensive—and, if possible, quantitative—analysis of a present or timeless situation will yield knowledge about temporal process. We must stop to consider, however, that men working in the historical life sciences or earth sciences do make use of ancient documents, though unwritten ones. If they could find written documents even hinting at some of the matters in which they are interested they would most certainly make use of them. Geologists, for example, have no such documents, and it is this circumstance that compels them to use other kinds of evidence and to rely on the supposition, following the doctrine of uniformitarianism, that past processes are like present processes. The student of human societies who compels himself to follow a similar procedure when a rich mine of written records are available is not just guided by a peculiar perversity or blind adoration for techniques followed in any study other than his own. In a larger measure he is driven to such strategy by the unexamined and untested assumption that a use of historical records will bar the way to science.

Another sort of shortcut around historical empiricism is suggested in the recent proposal by Karl Popper that we seek generalizations about "society" or "institutions" apart from the study of specific events. Appalled by the tragedy to which Europeans have been led by their devotion to Hegelian or Marxist philosophies of history, Popper is ready to accept the propositions "long ago brought out" that "history is interested in specific events rather than in general laws" and that whereas the study of events belongs to history the formulation of generalizations about society belongs to sociology.[44] Although he demonstates rather effectively that Marx was *not* historically empirical in reaching his laws of history, and though he does not hesitate to employ specific historical data in attacking many of Marx's propositions, Popper insists nevertheless that Marx's failure and the failure of historicism generally stems from the impossibility of generalizing about historical events. Yet he is interested in bringing knowledge, however derived, to bear on the problem of establishing and maintaining the "open society." He sees science as an attempt to explain the described events and things of our experience with the help of "universal laws." In social science, these are referred to as "sociological laws" or "natural laws of

[44] Karl R. Popper, *The Open Society and Its Enemies*, 2 vols. (London, 1947), II:251, 344–n. 7.

social life." The following hypothesis is offered as an illustration: "...wherever the freedom of thought, and of the communication of thought, is effectively protected by legal institutions and institutions ensuring the publicity of discussion, there will be scientific progress." We should not, however, speak of this as a historical law, Popper warns us. Similarly, in seeking the open society, he tells us, we can plan "institutions" but we cannot plan "history."[45]

The difficulties and contradictions in Popper's earnest and in many respects valuable historical commentary on the social implications of social science seem clear enough. Fearful of the consequences that have followed upon what he mistakenly regards as an attempt to make generalizations about men's historical experiences, he seeks, in effect, to withdraw institutions and society from history. He forgets that his sociological law of scientific progress must be derived from and tested by events in the experience of peoples before it can be used as a "universal law" for explaining events. There has been no communication of thought or protection of it outside of history, and general statements about these activities are generalizations about history or they are nothing. To be sure, such statements can differ markedly from the sort of historicist formulas that Popper attacks, but the difference should consist in the evidence they give of a closer attention to specific historical events rather than in their irrelevance to such happenings.

Popper has presented one of the clearest expositions of what is involved in a methodology that seeks the "nature" of an institution or culture element in its origin. He traces this procedure to the Greek belief that the nature of a thing *is* its origin or is determined by its origin, and he accounts in this way for the common conception that the task of social science is to explain social institutions by discovering their origins and their development flowing from such origins.[46] A vaguer awareness among anthropologists of the shortcomings of this orientation has been instrumental in the decision of many to forego earlier historical objectives while still retaining an interest in the "nature" of society or culture. The result here again is a peculiar discrimination between what is "in" history and what is not. Evans-Pritchard, for example, grants that historical study is not entirely unrelated to func-

---

[45] *Ibid.*, I:26, 56; II:306–n. 13, 132. Despite his opposition to historical "laws," it must be plain to any reader that Popper's work contains a rather elaborate philosophy of history. (See, for example, I:1; and for a philosophy of intellectual history, I:50–51.) That he prefers to call this merely an "interpretation" of history is beside the point; he offers it to men as a product of his study, and he urges them to act on it. This is not to make a point of the fact that Popper can be caught by his own criticism, but rather to suggest that he is compelled, like those he criticizes, to adopt a slippery theory of history by his refusal to approach history empirically.

[46] *Ibid.*, I:64.

tional study, but he insists that a knowledge of the history of an institution cannot tell us how it works or functions in social life.[47] "Working" or "functioning" of institutions are here regarded as somehow not historical phenomena. The specious distinction was more plainly made when Radcliffe-Brown called for a strict separation between a *"historical* interest in human life" and a "scientific understanding of the *nature* of culture and of social life"; and again when Lowie saw as an alternative to an interpretation of "unique series of events" the formulation of "general sociological principles . . . *independent of the time factor."*[48] Even in Kluckhohn's admirable study of Navaho witchcraft[49] the same uneasiness in the presence of what could be called history is evident. Kluckhohn felt it necessary to "specifically eschew" any historical analysis and chose to speak rather of the "dynamics of Navaho social organization" or, concretely, of the ways in which witchcraft affected Navaho society and individuals over a period of twenty years. Why such phenomena should be viewed as lying outside of history or why the sort of analysis he made of them should not be regarded as historical is not clear. To proceed as if dynamics, or structure, or function, or change, or movements, or trends can be found outside of history—outside of observed events or acts in time and place situations— is surely not what Kluckhohn and others are advocating. There is perhaps a suggestion here that *some* of the events or acts in history constitute "working" or "process" and other events or acts fall into a category of the accidental or unique. In any case, this shy skirting of the boundaries of history is motivated by conceptions of the nature of social phenomena that must stand as conclusions of study rather than unquestioned methodological postulates taken over from a past with which we are supposed to have broken.

It is obvious, of course, that in avoiding what is called historical study the object is often only to escape either the origin-hunting and grand developmental schemes of evolutionism or the special activities of narrative historians. Evolutionism and narration do not, however, exhaust the possible approaches to historical materials, and an identification of "history" with these two particular attitudes towards the temporal aspect of social experience is unwarranted. Such identification, taken in conjunction with the conviction that the loose procedures

---

[47] Evans-Pritchard, *op. cit.,* pp. 37–38, 60.

[48] Radcliffe-Brown, "The Present Position of Anthropological Studies," p. 9; Robert H. Lowie, *Primitive Society,* p. 436.

[49] Clyde Kluckhohn, *Navaho Witchcraft,* Papers of the Peabody Museum of American Archaeology and Ethnology, Harvard University, XXII, no. 2 (Cambridge, 1944).

of evolutionism are inadequate and the almost mystical notion that the absolute uniqueness of historical events and sequences render traditional historiography an artistic enterprise, leads either to abandonment of a scientific approach to the study of society or to procedures that imply a dimension to social life that lies outside the forbidding walls of history.[50]

The methodological impasse to which we are led here is attributable largely to the retention of old and misleading presuppositions about the "nature" of history. The continuing effects produced by this body of assumption in the study of man call for its reëxamination as a starting point for any endeavor to reach a new perspective for social science.

---

[50] There is mounting evidence that the former alternative is being chosen. Thus Evans-Pritchard is ready to call social anthropology an "art" (*op. cit.*, p. 85). Popper's assertion of the "simple fact that even if we observe today what appears to be a historical tendency or trend, we cannot know whether it will have the same appearance tomorrow" (*op. cit.*, II:81) reduces us, when we reflect upon it, to complete impotence in our efforts to learn from experience. Hayek's view that there are so many variables determining the results of any given social change that they cannot be comprehended by the human mind, and his reference to "spontaneous forces" in society ("Scientism...," *Economica*, 9:290, 11:29), have the same effect. Paul Radin's opinion that the only legitimate purpose of ethnology is to describe aboriginal cultures, followed in practice if not in theory by many of his colleagues, can lead only to abandonment of the once legitimately ambitious aims of his discipline. See his *Method and Theory of Ethnology* (New York, 1933).

CHAPTER VII

A PERSPECTIVE FOR SOCIAL SCIENCE

In their efforts to construct statements of social or cultural processes, social scientists have been and continue to be reluctant to utilize historical materials on a comparative basis and, consequently, by resorting to various unsatisfactory devices for establishing temporal relationships, they have supported untestable and hence persistent theories of change derived from analogy. The problem now confronting us is to discover means of utilizing the rich record of historical experience in the search for processes.

ALTERNATIVES TO NARRATION AND EVOLUTIONISM

A solution to this problem has occasionally been offered in the form of a plea that academic historians revise their traditional approach to the event content of experience.[1] Usually the suggestion is that historians enlarge the scope of their inquiries to include social, cultural, and economic history and then carry to this expanded subject matter the theoretical aims of social scientists. Although many historians have obviously already extended their interests beyond traditional political history, they have ordinarily refrained from extensive and systematic classification and comparison leading to generalizations and have claimed that their function is a special one, distinguishable from sociology, anthropology, political science, or economics.

There are recent signs, however, that historians are becoming pointedly aware of the contribution they might make as social scientists. In candid and searching reëxaminations of the aims of historical study, the Committee on Historiography of the Social Science Research Council[2] has pointed a way to new types of historical study that would involve explicit statement and testing of hypotheses. The emphasis on a need for more rigorous and open conceptualization and the clear recognition that historical investigation might begin with the recognition of a *problem* rather than a body of documents from which an account of "what actually happened" is to be reconstructed, are promising indications of a new and fruitful approach on the empirical-historical level.

Granting the merit of these proposals, however, it would be a serious

---

[1] The argument of Frederick J. Teggart (notably in his *Theory of History*) was directed, for example, principally to historians.

[2] *Theory and Practice in Historical Study*, Bulletin 54 (New York, 1946) and *The Social Sciences in Historical Study*, Bulletin 64 (New York, 1954).

mistake for scholars in the social science disciplines to assume that the methodological problems of humanistic inquiry in general are to be solved merely by reforms in academic historiography. And it would be a grievous tactical as well as strategic error for social scientists to suppose that they had a mission to perform in educating the poor misguided historian in the superior techniques and theoretical frameworks of the "scientific" disciplines.

Many historians make no secret of the fact that they seek an interpretation of the individual and unique aspects of the doings of particular peoples. They take as their special task the writing down of such interpretations. This writing follows a customary style, adherence to which raises perplexing problems of selection and synthesis. Narration has its own requirements, and, if they are to be met, the questions of subjectivism and relativism, present in any intellectual undertaking, assume peculiarly difficult forms. Historians struggle with these problems, and their skill is measured largely by their success in handling them. There is little point in telling them that they should classify their materials, search for regularities, organize their data along explicit theoretical lines, or formulate generalizations about history. There is little point in it because historians of this persuasion have made it clear that they are engaged in doing something quite different and intend to keep on doing it. A critic is no more justified in asking them to become sociologists than he would be in insisting that a landscape painter become an agronomist. We might, as citizens, deplore the consequences in human affairs when some historical interpretations are given weight their authors cannot claim for them. Or we might regret that men so well equipped for painstaking research do not sometimes focus their attention methodically on the general aspects of their hard-won information. But the fact remains that any one dissatisfied with what historians are doing has as his proper recourse the doing of something different.

When the question of doing something different is raised, however, it must be recognized that the problems associated with traditional historiography do not necessarily carry over. Historical study, broadly viewed, is not identical with the activities of the scholars we customarily call historians. They examine their data, on their own testimony, from a highly specialized point of view and utilize special procedures in dealing with it. The data do not dictate that point of view or procedure. "History-as-actuality" and "written history" are quite different things,[3] and the form followed by the latter neither exhausts the former nor

[3] See Charles Beard, in *Theory and Practice in Historical Study*, p. 12.

dictates its nature. What materials the historian selects from the record is determined by what he means to do with them: the extent to which subjective orientations affect his selection results partly from his resolve to devise an interpretative narrative. Given his objectives, he is undoubtedly correct in saying that a student of history must face this problem and acknowledge the limitations it places upon the kind of results he can achieve. But there is no reason for social scientists to be misled, or to mislead themselves, by the unwarranted conclusion that there are no alternatives to the historian's objectives and hence no escape from the serious methodological difficulties they entail.

It must also be acknowledged that the decision of some historians to concern themselves with what they see as the unique or singular in human experience provides no grounds for assuming that historical events are unique. If they see no generalities or processes in history, we must remember that they are not looking for them. Historians, then, can no more be regarded as qualified to pass judgment on the possibility of finding regularities in historical data than they can be blamed for not seeking regularities. Indeed, it might be said that scholars whose avowed purpose is to concentrate on the individual in history would be the least prepared to estimate the chances for making generalizations.

Actually, however, insistence upon the uniqueness of history is more often encountered among social scientists than among historians.[4] Often the historian is saying merely that his attention is focused on the unique in history; but the social scientist is ready to say that that is the *only* thing to see in history. There are probably few responsible historians who would censure a sociologist for trying to construct general propositions from an analysis of materials usually associated with the study of history—as long as the results are not called "history." If historians are occasionally skeptical of generalizations made about historical data, they are, with good reason, much more skeptical of generalizations reached without historical data. In any case, the belief among social scientists that historical happenings lie in the realm of the accidental, the spontaneous, or the fortuitous, and hence beyond the reach of science, cannot properly rest upon the testimony of historians.

Just as the problems of conventional historians should not be regarded as obstacles to historical social science, so the experiences of evo-

---

[4] The Committee on Historiography, for example, has specifically renounced the view that history is a scene of chance and uniqueness and has envisaged the possibility of classifying similar events (*The Social Sciences in Historical Study*, pp. 25–26, 95). Note, however, the persistent tendency to see history as composed of "particular events" or "unique historical situations," on the one hand, and "underlying trends" or "tendencies" or "processes," on the other (*ibid.*, pp. 97, 104). Does this dichotomy apply to "history-as-actuality"?

lutionists should not discourage us. The point must be reiterated here that the failure of sociologists and anthropologists to reach verifiable laws of institutional development is not a failure to generalize about observed or recorded historical experiences. We have seen, rather, that the sketching of evolutionary series proceeds in the absence of historical data. Events are specifically excluded, except for illustrative purposes, and their exclusion is based, moreover, on the supposition that events cannot be encompassed by scientific generalizations. Clearly, then, the belief that historical events are unique is a presupposition of evolutionistic studies, and it cannot be derived as a conclusion from critiques of those studies. The failure of evolutionism testifies to the impossibility of finding social processes outside of history, not in history.

Stripped of its association with the conventional study of history and the study of evolution, the concept of the uniqueness of historical events appears, as Edward W. Strong has said, to be merely one "whale of an assumption."[5] It can be supported only by vague appeals to man's free will and to similar notions concerning the baffling operation of contingency in history. It thrives in an atmosphere of ecstatic contemplation of the role played by Cleopatra's nose in human destiny. It is fed by fear of a determinism in history that might rob men of the freedom to shape their own lives. It survives because it carries with it the authority of antiquity, and because, like any idea long taken for granted, it escapes candid examination.

The conviction that events and sequences of events cannot be classified and compared without destroying what is real about them is not only unfounded; it is a debilitating assumption for social science. It stops inquiry by prejudging the results of a certain kind of investigation yet to be undertaken. In this sense, it begs a legitimate question. In Henry Thomas Buckle's words, "Those who affirm that the facts of history are incapable of being generalized, take for granted the very question at issue."[6] No profit for social science can result from assuming that we cannot find something before we look for it. It is equally clear, of course, that a belief in historical regularities is also an assumption. But this is an assumption that opens the way to inquiry and permits access to a body of materials that enforces an empirical orientation in studies of process.

When we discard the notion that time-place occurrences are unique it becomes possible to cut across the rigid alternatives of evolutionism and academic history and still retain a historical approach in social or

---

[5] Edward W. Strong, "How is Practice of History Tied to Theory?" *The Journal of Philosophy*, XLVI (1949) : 639.

[6] Henry Thomas Buckle, *History of Civilization in England* (New York, 1859–1861), I:5.

cultural study. Relieved of what Howard Becker has deplored as a "harsh insistence that historical data can be dealt with only idiographically,"[7] we can recognize that the shortcomings of evolutionism are not inherent in any effort to delineate social processes but only in an attempt to do so without the disciplined use of historical records. Then it becomes evident that the fundamental weakness of evolutionism does not reside in the special techniques used to establish chronological relationships among undated materials. The basic deficiency of this approach lies in acceptance of traditional views on the "nature" of history and the "unscientific" character of historical subject matter. It is this orientation that compels evolutionists to adopt an unfounded theory of social change with no specified empirical reference and to support it by converting spatial differences into temporal sequences with techniques allowable only on premises derived from the theory itself. To reject the whole project of scientific history on the grounds that these techniques are faulty is, indeed, to forget a goal because a wrong path has been taken. To surrender the historical objective because evolutionary hypotheses have been untestable or have not stood up under tests is to give up the search for realities because the quest for phantoms has been unrewarding.[8]

Criticism suggests, therefore, as a first step toward the formulation of testable statements of social or cultural processes, abandonment of the assumption that historical events are unique and acceptance of the assumption that there are discernible regularities in *all* historical occurrences.

The significance of this orientation toward the historical is apparent only if we recognize the disciplining effects on research that it imposes. It is not enough to say that all human experience is historical and, hence, if any generalizations are to be reached they must be historical

---

[7] Howard Becker, "Historical Sociology," in *Contemporary Social Theory*, ed. by Harry Elmer Barnes, Howard Becker, and Frances B. Becker (New York, 1940), p. 503.

[8] Anthropologists are on rather equivocal ground when they plead the nonhistorical character of their subject matter as an impediment to historical study or, at least, as a bar to the use of dated evidence. When we recall the early purpose of anthropology to arrive at a historical science of man and observe modern arguments for a "historical" anthropology, and when we note that nonliterate peoples without recorded histories were first studied just because of their supposed value as documents in reconstructing culture history, we might expect that anthropologists would abandon the study of primitives instead of the study of history once they came to feel that the two were incompatible. That such is not generally the case is no doubt explicable partly in terms of habitual preoccupation with a given subject matter and partly by the fact that new uses for ethnographic data have been found. But the extensive modern rejection of historical objectives among both anthropologists and sociologists (who are not traditionally committed to the study of primitives) would appear to stem rather from a reluctance to carry theoretical interests into the hazardous territory of historical events.

in the broadest sense. There is probably wide agreement on this proposition, but the meaning here attached to the term "history" is so general as to be pointless. Thus it is possible to accept such a view and still retain the idea that within the whole range of experience, call it historical if you will, some phenomena are obedient to law, and others—the historical in a more specific sense—are not. Adherence to this view can confuse the issue, however. The belief that some things come about by a series of happenings singular to each of them and other things come about by comparable or like processes, or even the belief that among common processes there will be some unique aspects, are conclusions that can be reached only through comparison; they are not warranted or serviceable as assumptions from which inquiry takes its departure.

Again, it is possible to agree that all experience is historical and yet to insist that there are two ways of conceiving experience, one of which focuses attention on the concrete and the other on the abstract. When social scientists take this stand, however, it seems that they often shift from the view that the abstract can be elicited from an analysis of experiences to the view that the abstract has an existence in experience independent of and apart from the concrete, and, therefore, that the general can or must be sought by avoiding attention to detail. They proceed as if social life consists of a mixture of general features and particular features and as if the task of the scientist is to see through or beyond the particulars and detect the general as one might sort through chaff to gather wheat. Hence the effort to seek the nature or functioning of society outside of social histories; hence the postulation of "forces" or "factors" in experience that produce or are responsible for observed happenings; hence the belief that process can be discovered in the essential nature of the entity undergoing process.

There is a tendency to forget here that if conceptions of social process do not result from reflection on observed occurrences in time and place, they result from adoption of analogies—in which case they are actually conceptions of biological or physical occurrences. The reference of conceptions to particulars might not always be explicit, for some specialists in social theorization leave the impression that their systems are called forth by a purely logical ritual that never allows empirical data to enter until a conceptual framework has been prepared for them. There is no denial, however, of the role of reflection or the imaginative intellect in asserting that conceptions, hypotheses, or generalizations are statements about particulars of which we are in some manner and degree aware.[9]

---

[9] See Charles Beard's observation that the social studies cannot be "independent, free-moving sciences." Abstractions must be checked against "comprehensive knowledge of the actuality of history." *Theory and Practice in Historical Study*, p. 10.

But a dilemma confronts us when we seek to dissociate conceptualization of historical processes from reflection on historical events. Acceptance of specific happenings, identified as to time and place, as material that can yield to generalization, releases us from this dilemma and, at the same time, performs a disciplinary service by compelling us to realize the scope of the empirical task involved in formulating and testing theories of how things work, or function, or come to be in societies and culture.

The assumption that we can generalize about historical events carries with it, then, injunctions against gratuitous distinctions between where this can and cannot be done, and against the various attempts to by-pass historical empiricism that we have examined. Positively, it involves acceptance of the proposition that social process is "an arrangeability in events."[10]

The decision to grapple with historical records for purposes of generalization clears the way for a radical alteration of the concepts and procedures of evolutionistic study. Perhaps the most basic result is removal of any compulsion to draw an analogy between social and biological change.[11] Access to a rich field of dated empirical materials clearly provides an opportunity and establishes an obligation to reach conceptions of process in this context rather than merely to impose on this domain the results of reflection by biologists on a quite different set of observations. Use of the biological analogy in any form and to any extent is unwarranted and dangerous. Considerations of the possible utility of analogical reasoning for conceptualization notwithstanding, the repeated experience of Western scholars over more than twenty-five hundred years demonstrates unequivocally that the analogy between society and an organism has worked uniformly to stop inquiry and to produce images of social process plainly contradicted by evidence at

---

[10] See S. Alexander, "The Historicity of Things," in *Philosophy and History*, ed. by Raymond Klibansky and H. J. Paton (Oxford, 1936), p. 12.

[11] The part played by the biological analogy in shaping current beliefs about social change should be grasped in historical perspective if our present difficulties are to be dealt with effectively. Considerable confusion on this point has arisen from two sources. First, there is a tendency to see this influence chiefly in terms of social Darwinism. The effort, however, to depict a struggle for existence, natural selection, and survival of the fittest in social process—i.e., to apply the mechanics of Darwin's theory of change in species to society—was relatively short-lived and unsuccessful. Second, anthropologists such as Boas and Kroeber have been quite properly concerned with combatting attempts to explain cultural phenomena by man's biological and psychological constitution. But neither biogenetic-psychogenetic theories of culture nor social Darwinism comprises the biological analogy between the growth of an individual organism and society. The oppression of biological thinking in the study of social and cultural phenomena has consisted chiefly in the conceptual identification of social process with organic growth process. See Kenneth E. Bock, "Darwin and Social Theory," *Philosophy of Science*, 22(1955):123–134.

hand. The belief derived from analogy that society is a process of slow and continuous change generated and directed by potential present within the thing changing from the beginning, has served only to divert attention from the evidence that must be admitted in any candid search for processes—evidence that cannot be dismissed as "secondary" factors or "unnatural" interventions or "anti-evolutionary" forces. Abandonment of the broader organic theory of change also carries with it a rejection of its subsidiary concepts. These include the notions that change has been always from the simple to the complex, from the homogeneous to the heterogeneous, or from the undifferentiated to the differentiated.

Since procedures in evolutionistic study are devised to circumvent the use of dated materials and can be applied only when the theory of change that they seek to illustrate has been adopted in advance, recognition of such materials as an appropriate subject matter for social science and relinquishment of the theory render these procedures both obsolete and indefensible. The practice of selecting social or cultural items, without attention to "times when and places where," and arranging them in an order that is supposed to represent a temporal developmental series, demands adoption of criteria of arrangement necessarily derived from the picture of change that the operation itself is supposed to prove. Discovery of the past in the present, of the temporal in the formal, of succession in coexistence, involves reliance upon some conception of what the past, the temporal, or the succession have been. That conception, if it is not based merely on analogy, is reliable and useful only to the extent that it is reached through a study of historical evidence. If the evidence is sufficient to warrant the conception there is no object in using it to justify a manipulation of spatial differences that can yield nothing but a temporal succession in keeping with the conception.

This really elementary critique of evolutionism can prove useful in reaching a perspective for the study of social processes if we accept its implications in full. Three basic points emerge.

First, the relation of hypotheses about social processes to their empirical reference should be so clear and specific that public testing with a definitely indicated body of data is possible. A hypothesis, although it is a general statement, can be of service only if its terms refer to the particulars about which it offers tentative generalization. If it is not to be merely an assertion inviting random illustration, a thesis to which selected materials can be fed, or a vague proposition supportable only by other propositions deduced from it, it must lead inquirers to a clearly specified universe of detail within which its refutation is possible. All this is commonplace, but if it be accepted together with a readiness to admit masses of recorded time-place acts or events as the matter to which statements of process refer and in the light of which they are to be tested, then the discipline imposed on the search for social processes is quite uncommon. In this atmosphere, talk about sociocultural movements from the simple to the complex, or from mechanical to organic solidarity, or from the ideational to the sensate raises staggering empirical problems. Given this orientation, the search for origins would probably be the last thing undertaken. Even with regard to relatively specific questions concerning, for example, the relation between communication and invention, or family disintegration and juvenile delinquency, the body of historical-empirical data to which these terms must be taken to refer sets a tremendous empirical task for anyone who would go beyond illustration and submit hypotheses to real tests. It is the historian's awareness of this that leads him sometimes to regard the bold generalizations of social scientists as altogether too facile. Arduous though the undertaking might be, it appears that if statements of social or cultural processes are to be raised above the level of interesting speculation, such statements must be submitted to tests by reference to the mass of concrete human experiences they seek to explain.

Second, a critique of evolutionism suggests that if a statement of process is to be tested and possibly refuted then we must guard against using procedures of verification suggested by assumptions implicit in the statement itself. We cannot, in other words, test a generalization by means that imply the truth of the generalization. This is what Tylor was doing when he used survivals to substantiate the developmental hypothesis, for survivals could be identified as such only upon acceptance of that hypothesis. So Spencer's data on undifferentiated and differentiated states of society became evidence for a temporal movement from the undifferentiated to the differentiated only when he assumed that such movement had taken place. And this is actually the case whenever a statement of process is documented by timeless items arranged in an order dictated by a presumption of what the process is. *There is a time order in any process, and time order, however indirectly it may be ascertained, must rest eventually on some means of time reckoning or dating.* To the extent that such basis is lacking, any arrangement of items to form a supposed successive series is permitted, and there are no grounds for accepting one and rejecting others.

This suggests the third point involved in a rejection of evolutionism, namely, that formulations of social or cultural processes must have reference to actual historical settings. Evolutionary schemes have been of two sorts: those that propose to depict a uniform course through which each social or cultural unit (tribe, people, nation) passes, and those that picture a single universal process in which all societies or cultures participate. Although these two objectives have by no means been differentiated in many evolutionistic studies, the distinction is sometimes made for purposes of defending a developmental thesis and rendering it immune to refutation.[12] Where the aim is to set down a sequence of stages through which every society or culture must pass, the result can be easily checked and overthrown by pointing to the historical experiences of some people for whom the alleged sequence does not hold true. But when the evolution sketched is of a single entity—Culture or Society—this checking by reference to examples of societies or cultures is impossible. Then the series becomes merely an arrangement of cultural differences that may or may not have chronological significance but which is, in either case, both meaningless and beyond verification because it has no reference to the life experience of any society of men.

Thus if we observe that a particular society is organized on the matriarchal principle and another on the patriarchal there are clearly no grounds in this for saying that there has been a development from the matriarchate to the patriarchate. Further, even if we establish the actual chronological priority of the matriarchate in this society to the patriarchate in the other, there is still no basis for asserting that the latter was once like the former. And then, if abstraction is carried so far as to say that in Social Evolution the matriarchate precedes the patriarchate we have simply lost touch with actual social experience and have postulated a hypothetical evolution of an artificial entity. Since the hypothesis does not refer to the histories of tribes or nations but only to a construct, it is impossible to test the hypothesis by reference to the particulars it is supposed to generalize. If we seek to establish the generalization that in human social experience patriarchate has succeeded matriarchate we can do so only by examining and comparing historical instances in which this has or has not taken place. If dated records bearing on the question are meager or lacking and we feel compelled to resort to other devices for determining chronology, we are obliged to bear in mind that however complicated these devices may become they must still be directed to establishing succession *in particular instances* which are then to be compared for purposes of generalization.

---

[12] A recent example may be found in the work of Leslie A. White, referred to in Chap. 6, note 10, above.

Examination and criticism of traditional conceptions of "history" and historical study conducts us, then, to a perspective that frees the social scientist from any obligation to avoid the specific, concrete, particular, time-place occurrences in human experience. Analysis of conventional theories of social change or evolution and methods of reaching such statements of social process yields a point of view from which the use of such data as raw material in the conceptualization of process becomes obligatory.

Revival of the Historical Orientation

There is mounting evidence of a wider acceptance of this perspective in recent years. The historical-mindedness of men as a trait that distinguishes them from other animals and the fact that no society can function without reference to the past are points that are reiterated in current literature.[13] It is emphatically recognized that "the world is a world of events,"[14] that "existence as we experience it is temporal," and that the world as we see it "has the character and the range of content and of diversity which it happens to have."[15] Going beyond a mere recognition of the historical dimension of human experience, it is now argued that the peculiar character of historical data does not preclude public, scientific handling. Introspection and intuition are challenged as the sole weapons that can be brought to bear in comprehending the "doings and sufferings" of peoples, tribes, and nations.[16] The way is opened to a rigorous, systematic, calmly rational exploitation of the specific records of men's experiences in times and places.

Promising signs of a willingness to accept the discipline imposed by a historical point of view are discernible in many quarters. Sociologists have been reminded by Karl Mannheim that simple description of the morphology of cultures is not enough, that differences must be explained in the light of background; in short, that there can be no "escape from historical empiricism."[17] At the Anglo-American Conference of Historians in 1931 the British sociologist, Ginsberg, challenged the old notion that history deals only with the singular and unique while social science concerns itself with universals. Arguing that sociological material is in its very nature historical and that even functional

---

[13] Joseph R. Strayer, "Introduction," in *The Interpretation of History*, ed. by Joseph R. Strayer (Princeton, 1943), p. 9.

[14] S. Alexander, *op. cit.*, p. 11.

[15] A. O. Lovejoy, *The Great Chain of Being* (Cambridge, Mass., 1936), pp. 329, 332.

[16] Edward W. Strong, "Fact and Understanding in History," *The Journal of Philosophy*, XLIV (1947) :623–624.

[17] Karl Mannheim, "German Sociology (1918–1933)," *Politica*, I (1934) :27.

analysis involves historical study, he pleaded for coöperation between historians and sociologists to the end of establishing a broader basis for comparative study of institutions. Ginsberg specifically rejected the notion that sociology and history differ in the kind of knowledge they seek.[18] Among American sociologists, Howard Becker has reminded us that as social scientists we cannot be restricted to a study of historyless preliterates or to contemporary happenings in our own civilization, but must reach out and tap the vast resources of the written record.[19] Anthropologists still interested in evolutionary processes in cultures are warned by Bidney that culture evolution and culture history must ultimately be the same, that "there can be no evolution of culture in general apart from the cultural history of given societies."[20] And to those anthropologists who would say that they are no longer interested in such questions, there are others who now reply that their discipline must interest itself in something beyond the unique, the exotic, or the nonrecurrent particulars, and look for generalizations at the temporal level.[21]

But a prodigiously laborious task is set those who would accept the implications of a thorough historical-empirical method and combine this with the lively theoretical interests of social science. Here the vast difference between the use of historical data for illustrative purposes and the actual testing of hypotheses by reference to the mass of relevant historical materials is so evident as to discourage, understandably, those who seek quick results in the study of man. It was just this circumstance that led the historically oriented Comte and Mill and Tylor to hope that there was some way of getting "around" or "behind" history and finding the treasure without doing the digging. Historians, with their realistic sense of just how detailed history is and how small the yield of painstaking research, are quick to warn us of the arduous path that must be trod by those who would seek anything like a science of history; and when this warning is coupled with the threat that the path will lead nowhere, it is not surprising that few set out.

There have been, however, in recent decades, those who made the effort, and we can profit from their experience. Although it might

---

[18] Morris Ginsberg, "History and Sociology," *Philosophy* (*The Journal of the British Institute of Philosophy*), 7(1932):442–445.

[19] Howard Becker, *op. cit.*, pp. 502–505. See also his "Constructive Typology in the Social Sciences," *ibid.*, pp. 17–46, and "The Field and Problems of Historical Sociology," in *The Fields and Methods of Sociology*, ed. by L. L. Bernard (New York, 1934), pp. 18–32.

[20] David Bidney, "On the So-Called Anti-Evolutionist Fallacy: A Reply to Leslie A. White," *American Anthropologist*, 48(1946):293.

[21] See Julian H. Steward, "Cultural Causality and Law: A Trial Formulation of the Development of Early Civilizations," *American Anthropologist*, 51(1949):1–27.

appear incongruous to mention the name of Spengler in the midst of a plea for a historical science of man, it must be granted that, whatever excesses he was guilty of, Spengler did launch a telling critique of traditional historiographic practice and suggest departures that have characterized subsequent inquiry in the field of cultural or civilizational history. In his attention to areas of human life ordinarily neglected by political historians, in his insistence on the plurality of histories, in his ridicule of the Europocentrism of Western scholars, and in his advocacy of a comparative study of cultures, Spengler demolished old idols and suggested, by precept if not by example, new perspectives in the study of human history.

Arnold J. Toynbee's work follows broad outlines that find an acknowledged parallel in Spengler. But in Toynbee there is more. In addition to the plural view of history and the comparative approach, *A Study of History* accepts the canons of scientific inquiry so disdainfully rejected by Spengler. Despite the theological overtones in Toynbee that some find so irksome, there is a tremendous effort here to bring large masses of empirical data to bear on explicitly formulated hypotheses. If Toynbee's theme is ponderous and his hypotheses elephantine to the point of unmanageability,[22] yet it cannot fairly be said that his generous conception of his task is taken by him as license to be vague or merely general. Toynbee can be refuted, rather than just maligned, by those who would go to the trouble.

The German sociologist Max Weber[23] displayed a similar willingness to accept histories as the context within which problems or theoretical questions are to be formulated and solutions sought. Although dressed in a somewhat cumbersome methodology that seems at times to be designed more to forestall objections to a transgression of customary lines between historical and scientific study than to facilitate inquiry, Weber's substantive research again serves as a model of what can be accomplished when specific time-place social phenomena are identified

---

[22] Cf. *The Social Sciences in Historical Study*, p. 28. The point that many of Toynbee's theories are "nonoperational" is well taken, but this is a defect in technique and does not destroy the value of his work as an example of a comparative study of histories.

[23] For a statement of Weber's methodological position see *Max Weber on the Methodology of the Social Sciences*, trans. and ed. by Edward A. Shils and Henry A. Finch (Glencoe, Ill., 1949). Significant portions of Weber's extensive writings are now available in English translation. See *General Economic History*, trans. by F. H. Knight (London, 1927); *The Protestant Ethic and the Spirit of Capitalism*, trans. by Talcott Parsons (London, 1930); *From Max Weber: Essays in Sociology*, trans. by H. H. Gerth and C. Wright Mills (New York, 1946); *Max Weber: The Theory of Social and Economic Organization*, trans. by A. M. Henderson and Talcott Parsons (New York, 1947); *The Religion of China: Confucianism and Taoism*, trans. by H. H. Gerth (Glencoe, Ill., 1951); *Ancient Judaism*, trans. by H. H. Gerth and Don Martindale (Glencoe, Ill., 1952).

and related through comparative studies. Though the problems that Weber set himself are much narrower in scope than the sweeping projects of Spengler or Toynbee, once Weber sought an understanding of even limited situations in actual historical contexts he was committed to a breadth of investigation and an attention to voluminous detail quite unusual in the discipline in which he holds so distinguished a place.

The researches of Frederick J. Teggart and Margaret T. Hodgen[24] reveal in striking fashion the possibilities open to those who dare to classify supposedly "unique" events and seek explanations of them in terms of other classes of happenings. Hodgen's work on technological changes in England is particularly instructive as an example of the kind of labor involved for social scientists, as well as the kind of results to be expected, once they forsake speculation about change and undertake a comparative analysis of changes evidenced by historical records.

Further examples of a new historical perspective in social science are to be found, at long last, in the productions of some venturesome anthropologists. Having decided that anthropology should be "historical" and that culture processes are to be discerned in the "complication of events," they have directed their attention to peoples, times, and places about which there is historical information and with regard to which the events are not entirely hypothetical. A. L. Kroeber[25] is a case in point. Although showing a certain self-consciousness and some trepidation about moving into a new field, Kroeber, it could be argued, found out more about culture processes in his *Configurations* than the entire preceding century of anthropological speculation yielded. By accepting specific dated and sited events as somehow alike and hence subject to classification as to kind, time, and space, he has set problems for the student of culture that promise a radically new departure in research. In another area of anthropological study, acculturationists[26] have, by the very statement of their problem, been compelled to turn their attention to the "laboratory" of history for light on the question of what goes on when peoples or cultures meet and affect one another. And here again, once the phenomenon envisaged by the concept of acculturation is encountered on the historical scene the plurality of its

---

[24] Frederick J. Teggart, *Rome and China: A Study of Correlations in Historical Events* (Berkeley, 1939); Margaret T. Hodgen, *Change and History* (New York, 1952).

[25] A. L. Kroeber, *Configurations of Culture Growth* (Berkeley, 1944).

[26] See Melville J. Herskovits, *Acculturation, the Study of Culture Contact* (New York, 1938); *Man and His Works* (New York, 1948), chap. 31 and literature cited there.

occurrence becomes manifest and the way is clear for that comparison of histories advocated by Boas in 1896.[27]

Conclusion

The perspective evident in such recent works as the above, different though they may be in their procedural techniques and their immediate objectives, can now be summed up as follows:

The Acceptance of Histories.—What is involved here is the idea that dated and sited acts, events, or happenings in human experience, of whatever sort, and largely available to us in written records, are data with which social scientists must work in their own way. They are not the exclusive property of historians; they can be used for purposes other than the construction of historical narratives.

If the objective of social scientists is to reach testable generalizations about human social life, acceptance by them of historical data implies the working assumption that these discrete, specific, individual data can be classified, that they are "generalizable" data, and that the generalizing operation in social science must cope with them.[28] To say that as soon as we classify events we take them out of context and so destroy their "historical" character is allowable only from the point of view of the traditional academic historian whose special use of events, does, indeed, preclude classification.[29] But to classify events, to deny their uniqueness, to generalize about them, is only to pursue objectives other than those of narrative historians. To do so is not to distort "nature" or to violate any supportable rule of inquiry.

Acceptance of histories by social scientists further implies the acceptability of *all* historical materials relating to human experience. There are no grounds for assuming that some historical data can be handled

[27] For examples of the contributions of historians proper to the kind of study referred to in this section, see *The Social Sciences in Historical Study,* chaps. 4–6; see also Louis Gottschalk, *Understanding History* (New York, 1950).

[28] Generalities are not found in nature. It is misleading to speak as Sapir did of "generalized events." See Edward Sapir, *Time Perspective in Aboriginal American Culture, a Study in Method.* Canada Department of Mines, Geological Survey, Memoir 90, No. 13, Anthropological Series (Ottawa: Government Printing Bureau, 1916). [Reprinted in *Selected Writings of Edward Sapir* ... (Berkeley, University of California Press, 1949), pp. 389–462.] "While the importance of individual events and personalities for the progress of human affairs is not to be underestimated, the historical reconstructions of the cultural anthropologist can only deal, with comparatively few exceptions, with generalized events and individualities." (P. 3.)

[29] Cf. Robert E. Park and Ernest W. Burgess, *Introduction to the Science of Sociology* (Chicago, 1921), p. 8: "As soon as historians seek to take events out of their historical setting, that is to say, out of their time and space relations, in order to compare them and classify them; as soon as historians begin to emphasize the typical and representative rather than the unique character of events, history ceases to be history and becomes sociology."

scientifically while others cannot, or that there are, in the nature of things, both general and unique elements in history.[30] The general is not a quality of the variety of experience as such; it is a tentative conception shared by investigators in their efforts to make sense of the apparently random particularity of the experience. To divide experience into the general and the unique and make this a basis for separate disciplinary approaches to the study of society divorces social science generalizations from their empirical universe.

Systematic use of dated materials by social scientists also involves confidence in the reliability of historical records. The belief that what men have observed and recorded about human social life is but a distorted, subjective reflection of what was really there is a debilitating assumption. This sort of skepticism jeopardizes the entire study of man, for not only does it deny us access to the great bulk of human experience, but it also eventually casts doubt upon the reliability of all observation. For all recorded observations were at one time "contemporary," and there is little warrant for the current conceit that the intelligent and careful observer is an exclusively modern phenomenon. The bright-eyed young sociologist armed with his scheduled interview might generously concede that the shrewd perceptions of a Hesiod, Machiavelli, or Voltaire deserve a place, alongside his own findings, in the broad fund of social knowledge. All records call for careful scrutiny, but the techniques devised by historians for establishing the reliability of their data are by no means inferior to those employed by the social sciences.

Resistance by social scientists to the use of history is also based, in more recent years, on the argument that what went on in the past is irrelevant to present problems. It is clear, of course, that only certain historical experiences are relevant to certain problems that we attack, that the historical contexts of social life vary in both time and space. But we must be very careful in denying the relevancy of past to present experience or we can be reduced to the idiot's approach to life, where each succeeding instant is new and without precedent and intelligent conduct gives way to random groping. We can not afford to stop with an appreciation of the uniqueness or singularity of historical experiences. If we are to approach the future with anything more than the blankness of amnesia, we must rather search for what is common in apparently multifarious experience. And in ranging through time in search of precedent no prejudgment as to the relevancy of near or dis-

---

[30] The assumption of such a division was made, for example, by Durkheim in his preface to the first issue of *L'Année Sociologique*, I (1896–97) :i–vii. See comment by Robert H. Lowie, *History of Ethnological Theory* (New York, 1937), p. 198.

tant past is admissible. The proper study of man is the study of man everywhere, at all times.

Finally, the acceptance of histories does not imply for social science a concern with origins or an obsession with the long-ago. Some historians have claimed that good historical narration requires that the writer be a certain distance from his subject if the proper tone is to be preserved, and this, coupled with our school-days recollection of history as always dealing with remote occurrences, produces in our minds a picture of the antique whenever the word history is used. Also, because eighteenth- and nineteenth-century "historical" sociology and anthropology were almost exclusively occupied with a search for origins, any suggestion that we return to a historical perspective might seem to imply a revival of that undertaking. But history is a word properly applicable to all of man's social experiences, and experience, once we know of it, is always past experience, whether it occurred yesterday or a thousand years ago. To think of experience as historical, then, is not to direct one's attention to the dim recesses of time. It is simply to accept the largest amount of evidence possible for constructing and testing propositions about how things work in social life, and it is to see this evidence in all its rich and precise detail, fixed as to time and place, and specific as to the human beings involved. Thus the acceptance of histories has a disciplinary effect on our efforts to formulate generalized statements about social life that can be applied with some confidence to real life situations.

Comparison of Histories.—Having accepted history in the above sense, the crucial question arises as to what we do with it. If what happened in history is regarded as subject matter for social science, how is that subject matter to be organized, manipulated, and utilized, in order to reach generalizations?

The sort of understanding that we call "scientific" comes from systematic examination of more than one instance of the thing or sequence of occurrences about which we seek to generalize. Scientific knowledge is yielded, in other words, by comparison. We know a thing by virtue of seeing it as being of a kind with others. Hence the common scientific observation that given a thing of this *kind,* placed in a situation of this *kind,* this *kind* of result can be expected. Generalizations refer to particulars, and it is by comparison of particulars that we reach generalizations.

It is perhaps banal to observe that the scientist proceeds by comparing many occurrences of a phenomenon identified by progressively refined criteria. But if we proceed on the assumption that specific happenings in the social life of peoples are the subject matter of social science, that these happenings are not unique, that they can be grouped or bunched or classified into kinds, then the implications of this commonplace for social science are far-reaching and not immediately evident. For we are compelled to recognize that when we say Society, Culture, Family, Law, War, Painting, Parliamentarism, Imperialism, Division of Labor, or Magic we are naming distinct congeries of events or acts discernible in the experiences of many particular peoples in many particular places and times, or we are naming nothing. Moreover, given this viewpoint, we are obliged to see that if we would relate War to Imperialism or seek to establish some causal nexus between them, we are again relating classes of time-place events, or we are relating nothing.

Taking revolutions as an example of a crudely conceived kind of event sequence, Salvemini has given us a simplified statement of what is involved in finding regularities in social experience: "To determine whether revolutions are governed by constant laws, there is only one method: we must compare one with the other the greatest possible number of revolutions ... and we must see whether between these phenomena so far apart in time and space there can be discovered similarities or dissimilarities which are constant."[31]

While this might appear at first glance to be a rather naïve or empty directive for social science, it will not be so if the full disciplinary effects of the comparative-historical framework are kept in mind. In the light of the requirements it imposes, it is clear beyond equivocation that the probable validity of any proposition in social science depends directly upon the extent and detail of observed experience with which it accords. Escape from historical empiricism is cut off, and the naïveté in stopping in social science with statements that "history can be made to show" is clearly exposed.

Before histories can be compared, it is, of course, necessary to view history as plural. There are many histories, not just of tribes, nations, or peoples, but of arts and sciences and religions and technologies. Moreover, we need to think of histories as not only accounts of what happened in traditional areas of inquiry but as identifiable sequences of occurrences.[32] Thus, what happens when a number of persons is formed

---

[31] Gaetano Salvemini, *Historian and Scientist* (Cambridge, Mass., 1939), pp. 29–33.

[32] V. Gordon Childe's argument that the number of "instances" available for comparative treatment is too limited to allow any conclusions is hardly tenable. In the first place, Childe seems to have in mind as "instances" the vast ages of archaeology, or at least the whole sweep of civilizations. Histories can be conceived in shorter terms. Second, the social scientist must, after all, make the best of the data he has; if the data are sparse, the solution does not lie in disregarding them. Childe's contention that the instances are not "genuinely independent" is apparently a reflection of his evolutionistic bias. That one society has been influenced by another does not

into a rioting mob constitutes a history, of which there are, we assume, many instances. By comparing what happens in many such "little histories" we can come to some general statement about mob formation. Again, whatever it might be that we seek to associate with the rise of a mob must first be observed as a series of concrete happenings that also constitute a history, of which, we assume, there are many instances.

Social scientists quite commonly conduct studies along these lines, using a number of instances to detect variables and hold certain factors constant, but they seldom regard such research as historical in character simply because they are accustomed to distinguishing historical research by its result in narration or by the particular procedures and aims of academic historians. The unfortunate result is that social scientists both restrict the scope of human experience which they investigate and fail to recognize that whether it be called "case study," or "intensive analysis," or "crucial experiment," or "history," the same attention to the complicated particulars of social life is required and the same relation between extent of observation and generality of conclusion must prevail.

In other cases the "historical" approach seems to convey to social scientists a notion of grandiose attempts to sketch the broad sweep of social or cultural development through time. This is simply to identify any interest in a theoretically oriented comparison of histories with old evolutionist objectives. An outlook that sees history as plural and envisages classifiable event sequences as comparable items can direct inquiry to specific problems rather than to the elucidation of a comprehensive philosophy of history.[33]

The comparative approach rests on the assumption that there are comparables in history. This assumption, which denies the absolute individuality of events and sequences, is justified not only by its function in opening the way to a search for uniformities and thus generalizations, but also by the fact that it releases us from the ancient and persistent dependence on analogies between social and biological or mechanical phenomena. When social life is conceived in terms of unique wholes, or entities, or processes, comparison is impossible. In this situation, men have repeatedly resorted to analogy as a specious form of comparison. But when analogy is abandoned, comparison is always involved in arriving at generalities. The issue is whether comparison

---

prevent the search for regularity in historical process except when we assume that typical change is always the result of potency within the society. See Childe's *History* (London, 1947), pp. 2–3, 63.

[33] See *The Social Sciences in Historical Study,* pp. 100–101.

will be explicit and thorough at the level of detail, or merely suggestive and illustrative.

The Function of Hypothesis.—In making comparisons, we conceptually put certain things or events together as like, and we seek to explain their occurrence or working in terms of their common association with certain other things or events. These operations obviously imply the presence of ideas about what "goes together" or what is significantly related to something else. When such ideas are stated in systematic form, or when they are observed to exercise a systematic influence on the operations, they are called hypotheses.

One of the most vexing problems of the social as well as the other sciences is how an investigator comes by hypotheses that will be useful in promoting inquiry and reaching testable conclusions. Sometimes the point of this question is blunted with the argument that neither the source nor the apparent intrinsic usefulness of a hypothesis need be considered, that what is important about a hypothesis is whether or not it works, and that plenty of hypotheses lie about for the taking, ready to start any inquirer on his way either to a solution of his problem or to the construction of a new hypothesis.

The issue is germane to the present discussion on only two counts. First, it may be suggested that a merely random selection of hypotheses for testing is not an economical procedure in research, nor is it one that scholars habitually follow. Hypotheses do lie about for the taking, but as a matter of fact a given investigator selects one and not others, and he is guided by certain considerations in so doing. Foremost among the influences bearing upon his choice is what he knows of the experiences of other scholars in their use of certain ideas. This is an entirely proper influence and one that should be sharpened by careful examination of the course of previous inquiry and the ideas that shaped it. The scientific ideal notwithstanding, misleading or false hypotheses do not automatically drop by the wayside when the data do not support them. They have a way of persisting, and they are sustained by many devices besides corroborative evidence. Hence we are obliged to inspect continually the heritage of ideas that lie about us for the purpose of detecting both worn-out themes and promising leads. The uses of ideas in all fields of inquiry have histories, and we can learn from the experience that study of these histories will yield us.

The present study, for example, would suggest that the persistent idea that historical events are unique or that experience is divisible into natural and accidental categories is not a useful notion and that a quite contrary view might profitably be taken. In a more substantive sense, the study discloses that in the investigation of social and cultural processes the idea that these entities or their components naturally change in a slow and continuous fashion has not served inquiry well, for it has turned the attention of men away from the conditions under which changes occur and concentrated it upon what were regarded as obstacles to change. It can be suggested, therefore, that we attend to hypotheses that direct inquiry to phenomena of stability or stagnation, or that point to intercourse, borrowing, and specific contacts between peoples and their effects, or that consider the role of comparable key events in initiating changes, or that explore the varying tempo of changes in relation to certain kinds of happenings.

The second point has to do with the context of substantive information in which hypothesizing goes on. Hypotheses are in some sense, no doubt, products of the imaginative intellect. To formulate a new idea, to see a hitherto unnoticed relationship, to "pick up the other end of the stick"—these are creative acts. But just how to *be* creative or imaginative, just how to "see" in a new way, are things about which we know very little. The mechanics of creativity, if there be such, remain a mystery. Yet we do know something of the conditions under which men have been creative. Among these conditions, a broad awareness of the world of events, acts, and things seems to be a prime factor. If inspiration depends on some mysterious indwelling faculty, it remains that this faculty manifests itself only with those individuals who are keenly aware of some part of their world. Fruitful thinking takes place in an atmosphere of information, and although we seek information always with the guidance of abstract ideas the evidence for a reciprocal relationship between the two is impressive.

We return, therefore, to the social scientist's dependence on historical empiricism.[34] There is no empirical ladder to hypothesis, but the system builder in social theory needs other materials besides a grasp of logic and a well-disciplined mind. Although some notable theorizers in the social and natural sciences have not been particularly industrious observers, we should not be deceived into thinking that they have not used the ideas and observations of others. Creation of hypotheses or of systems of theory about society or culture must always proceed against a background of accepted information—correct or incorrect—about societies or cultures, whether this is acknowledged by the theorist or

---

[34] *Ibid.*, pp. 131–132: "... recognition of a problem starts *from knowledge*, not from a random decision to study something. ... Theoretical schemes and working hypotheses, even if not selected on the basis of certain knowledge, need not be selected at random."

not. Our success in this area depends in large part, therefore, upon the thoroughness and extent of our awareness of the historical world.

◇   ◇   ◇   ◇   ◇   ◇

What might appear to be the radical boldness of these proposals for historical science should be tempered with the realization that both "history" and "science" are used here in a somewhat modified sense.

Historical study has been traditionally conceived by social scientists in rather sweeping genealogical terms. Usually it suggests a search for the coming-to-be of society, culture, or institutions from remote beginnings and through the broad reaches of time. It is customarily supposed to aim at the construction of elaborate developmental or evolutionary sequences, cyclic phases, or other expansive patterns of change. Such aims were characteristic of the great eighteenth- and nineteenth-century efforts to depict how things have come to be as they are, and the dream is by no means dead today. An ambition to sum things up, to seek the general course of things, to place one's total present in a context of the temporal cosmos, is a worthy one, especially when the attempt is made along empirical lines, as in Toynbee's case. But the proposal here is a more modest one. Historical studies can be specific—a matter of seeking to determine in rigorous fashion what kinds of happenings have been significantly associated with what other kinds of happenings in the experiences of men. What, for example, might have been the common antecedents of peaceful settlements of disputes between nations, and how might we view these to reach useful explanations or understandings of the conditions of peace? What, if any, have been the common experiences of peoples when they have enjoyed efflorescences in the arts or sciences? What can be found in the doings of men that is associated with the fluctuations of crime rates in American cities? Problems of this sort are familiar to social scientists, but they are not usually thought of as questions calling for historical investigation. All a historical perspective does is recall to us that we cannot attack such problems either by juggling bloodless concepts of change, mobility, class, human nature, or disorganization, or by myopic analyses of presumably crucial cases. Sooner or later the richly varied world of concrete experiences must be accepted and struggled with and conceptually subdued. To see human social life as it *happens* to be is historical-mindedness.

And so with science. The belief that a science of human affairs is impossible because of the nature of its subject matter rests upon a number of outrageous assumptions. Foremost among these is the notion that science is identified by its mathematical exactness. This is to miss the whole import of the scientific revolution in Western thinking, for the adoption of a scientific attitude involves abandonment of the pursuit of exactness. The precision of absolute truth may be sought in theology or in philosophy of history; but science thrives on inexactitude. Its propositions must be continually refuted or the enterprise is finished. Scientists make statements of probability, and although they use these as working hypotheses, a constant proviso is that they are improbable. Taking a scientific attitude implies satisfaction with successive approximations, not an insistence upon exactness. The picture of science as a goblin that would swallow the humanity in man and digest his hopes and fears, loves and hates, doings and sufferings into mathematical formulas rests on an outworn conception of science.[35] This picture has done much mischief in the social studies, not so much by driving those who would be scientific to a sole reliance upon measurement techniques, but by releasing others from the common standards of evidence and public testing associated with scientific work.

The conviction that social phenomena do not conform to "iron laws" is no excuse for abandoning the search for regularities in historical experience. Nor is it justification for denying this pursuit the name of science or exempting students of society from the requirement that their generalizations have explicit, testable reference to a specified body of particulars. A retreat into undisciplined intuitionism is a last resort for men who have failed to cope rationally with the problems of social living; it is not a proper point of departure in the study of man.

Our situation is such that we *must* hope that we can find some regularities in histories to guide us on our perilous way. In making the search we should remember that "by far the greatest obstacle to the advancement of the sciences, and the undertaking of any new attempt or department, is to be found in men's despair and the idea of impossibility."

---

[35] "The very concept of nature in opposition to which Dilthey proclaimed his *Geisteswissenschaft* has long been abandoned by the scientists themselves, and the notion of a description of nature which indiscriminately subjects men and their fates like rocks and stones to its 'unalterable laws' survives only as a nightmare of certain historians." Edgar Wind, "Some Points of Contact between History and Natural Science," in *Philosophy and History*, p. 256.

INDEX